*To Donna
Blessings*

Dick Browning

EXPLAINING TEXAS

By

Dick Browning

All Rights Reserved

Copyright 2011

ISBN 978-1-4276-3511-2

To my wife Jan

Table of Contents

EXPLAINING TEXAS	7
GIANT BOAR	10
CLOVIS PEOPLE	11
ALVAREZ DE PINEDA	12
CABEZA DE VACA	13
LaSALLE	16
TEXAS UNDER SPANISH RULE	18
THE NUN IN BLUE	19
MYSTERY WOMAN	21
BRIT BALEY	23
JOSIAH WILBARGER	25
THE AUSTIN COLONY	27
MUSTANG	28
AN EARLY RODEO	30
JAMES BOWIE	31
SEEDS OF REBELLION	34
THE TEXAS REVOLUTION	36
PRESIDIO LA BAHIA	38
THE BATTLE OF THE ALAMO	40
HOUSTON TAKES COMMAND	42
THE YELLOW ROSE OF TEXAS	45
TEXAS NAVIES	47
THE REPUBLIC OF TEXAS OPEN FOR BUSINESS	49
THE GREAT RAID OF 1840	51
TEXAS RANGERS	54
TEXAS RANGER CAPTAIN L. H. MCNELLY	57
1840 FRONTIER	60
RANGER ALEXANDER WALLACE	61
JACK HAYS, TEXAS RANGER	63
CYNTHIA ANN PARKER & QUANAH	65
GERONIMO	68
TEXAS JOINS THE UNION – MEXICAN WAR	70
GALVESTON	72
CIVIL WAR	74
RECONSTRUCTION	77

EMANCIPATION PROCLAIMATION	79
CATTLE DRIVES	80
TEXAS COWBOY BOOTS	83
JOHN HARDIN, BILL LONGLEY, DOC HOLLIDAY,	85
OUTLAW BELLE STAR	88
LA REUNION	90
LAW WEST OF THE PECOS	92
OLD RIP	96
FRENCH WINE HAS A TEXAS FLAVOR	98
DR PEPPER	99
TEXAS RAILROADS	100
ROSS PEROT	102
TEXAS OIL	105
UFO	109
TEXAS LUMBER INDUSTRY	110
1900 GALVESTON HURRICANE	112
FIRST POWERED FLIGHT	114
MILITARY AVIATION BORN IN TEXAS	115
TEXAS WEATHER	117
BURIED TREASURE	119
THE GREAT DEPRESSION	123
RED RIVER BRIDGE WAR	124
TEXAS PRISON RODEO	126
WRONG WAY CORRIGAN	127
TEXAS WON WWII	129
HELIUM	132
A NEW KIND OF BURIED TREASURE	134
DEL RIO RADIO	135
TEXAS IS A STATE OF MIND	137
ANNA NICOLE SMITH	139
REPTILES	141
BLUEBONNETS	146
FERAL HOGS	147
CADDO LAKE	149
LOVING COUNTY	153
SHERIFF JESS SWEETEN	154
TEXAS HAS ITS OWN POWER GRID	157

TEXAS INDEPENDENCE..158

Texas is a state of mind. Texas is an obsession. Above all, Texas is a nation in every sense of the word. And there's an opening convey of generalities. A Texan outside of Texas is a foreigner.

John Steinbeck

EXPLAINING TEXAS

Years ago I was in a village in the "Green Hell" of Brazil's Mato Grosso. It wasn't the end of the world, but you could see it from there. The missionary knew a little English. He asked me where I was from. I told him, but he couldn't understand me. I showed him the charm on my key chain in the shape of Texas. He recognized it immediately. He asked why I wasn't wearing cowboy boots and a Stetson hat. He said he would have expected me to be taller.

When God made the world, he carved out a special land men call Texas. Texas is recognized around the world and who wouldn't wish to be a Texan?

For three hundred years Spain was unable to tame Texas. The violent horse Indians of the plains ruled the land and would not cede an inch of it. They had taken it from those who came before who had taken it from those who came even earlier.

In the end, the Spanish/Mexicans opened Texas up to anyone bold enough to try to settle it. To understand Texans, you must understand, it took a special breed in early days to even consider coming to Texas. They were courageous and fiercely independent. Many came running from the law. Many came to escape too much law. Those who brought their families were expected to take care of them without interference or help from the government. As Texans molded the land to their own unique vision, Texas molded the Texans.

In addition to their many admirable traits, Texans tend to be insufferably boastful. They will tell you not to ask a man if he is from Texas. If he is, he will tell you. If he is not, don't embarrass him by asking.

Texas is big. Before joining the Union it was even bigger, but even today it is huge. Try to walk across it from East to West and it will take you months and several pairs of shoes. If you make it at all, you will have walked a third of the way across America.

Texas is deserts in the west, thick forests in south and east, rugged mountains in the Big Bend, and vast prairies. Texas has ranches bigger than some eastern states.

Texas can become an independent republic again any time the voters choose. This was a stipulation when we joined the United States. We are the only state that can fly our flag at an equal height as the American flag.

Texas is large herds of cattle and miles of crops.

Texas is breathtaking fields of bluebonnets every spring in its hill country.

Texas is 186 men in the Alamo defiantly standing up in the cause of freedom to Santa Anna's army of thousands.

Texas is cowboys battling Indians, rustlers, and weather, herding longhorns up the Chisholm Trail.

Texas is wildcatters getting fabulously rich overnight in the oil fields only to lose it next year in a series of dry holes.

Texas is Rangers fighting Indians and hanging horse thieves where they catch them.

Texas is bass fishing in the lakes, tubing down the river in the hill country or surfing on over 300 miles of Gulf beaches.

Texas is the stuff of myth and legend.

Over two hundred sixty years after Harvard was established we were still shooting Indians down here in Texas.

Texas is Friday night high-school football, Saturday college football, Sunday professional football and don't forget the Dallas Cowboys' Cheerleaders, and the Kilgore Rangerettes.

Texas is being proud just to say you are a Texan.

GIANT BOAR

I received an E-mail claiming this oversized wild hog was shot outside of Conroe, Texas. On further investigation, it turns out it was not in Texas at all. Why would anyone promote a lie like that? I could only conclude it was probably some Texan who couldn't stand the thought that any creature so outlandish could exist anywhere but Texas. We Texans do have a tendency to boast.

We tell the story of the Texan who went to Alaska after it joined the Union. They claimed it was now largest state. While there, he listened to them boast of their 3.197 named natural lakes, three million unnamed natural lakes, and a hundred thousand glaciers. He came home to Texas and told his friends Texas is still the largest state above water.

If you go to Google and type in TEXAS LIARS CONTESTS, you can find out where the closest liars contest is in Texas.

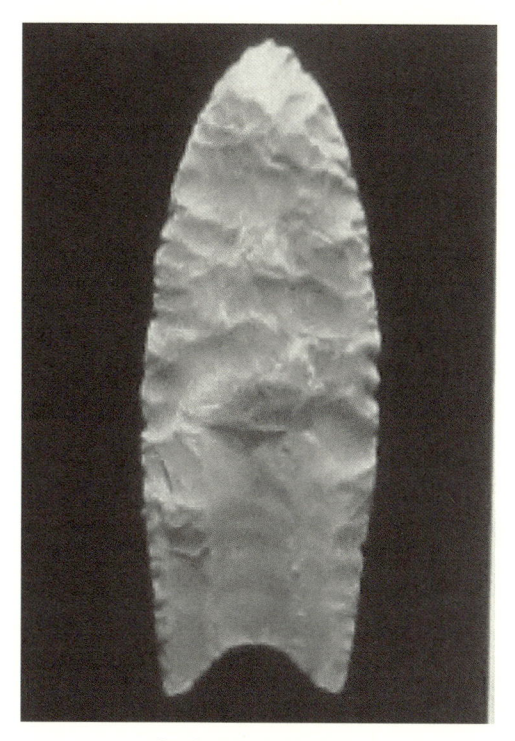

CLOVIS PEOPLE

Forty miles north of Austin, Texas, you will find the Gault Dig. Is is the site for the center of study of the Clovis peoples who are thought to be the earliest settlers of the western hemisphere. There is a large flint deposit there that provided a major tool making facility going back as far as thirteen thousand years. The characteristic Clovis spear point was used to hunt mammoths, horses, and bison at the end of the last ice age. The spear points have been found in all forty eight contiguous states, up into Canada and down into South America, but nowhere else in the concentration of those in Texas. Sixty percent of all Clovis artifacts are found in Texas. Texans conclude from this that for the past thirteen thousand years, six out of ten people prefer to live in Texas.

I have moved over a great part of Texas and I know that within its borders. I have seen just about as many kinds of country, contour, climate and conformation as there are in the world.

Author John Steinbeck

ALVAREZ DE PINEDA

The first European to set foot on the hallowed ground of Texas was Alvarez de Pineda who in 1519 mapped the Gulf coast from Florida to Tampico. This was only 27 years after Columbus discovered the New World and eighteen years before Cabeza de Vaca got to Texas. He spent forty days exploring the area around the mouth of the Rio Grande while his crew made ship repairs. The reason why Cabeza de Vaca is remembered and Alvarez is not is that the former wrote extensively extolling his adventures in Texas while Alvarez, when he got to Tampico, got cross wise with the local Aztecs who killed and ate him. As my former boss in the navy, Commander Jogan, once told me, *He who tooteth not his own whistle, shall forever remain in a state of untootedness.*

CABEZA DE VACA

Growing up in Texas, we all learned Texas History or at least were subjected to it. The history book told us about Cabeza de Vaca who with three other guys were the first Europeans to explore Texas. They were part of an expedition of 400 conquistadors who left Spain in 1537 to colonize the Gulf coast from Florida to Mexico.

Arriving at Tampa Bay, Florida, they want inland and tangled with the natives, swatted mosquitoes, and starved for several months before reaching Apalachee Bay with only 242 survivors.

The ships that brought them had abandoned them and walking around inland wasn't working. They melted down their spurs and other metal objects to make tools to build five primitive boats then went west sailing along the Gulf coast. When they reached the Mississippi River, the current swept them out to sea where they were ravaged by a hurricane.

Two boats with forty men eventually wrecked on Galveston Island. They used the last of their clothes to plug the leaks in their boats only to lose them in a storm.

Local natives befriended them, thinking them some sort of gods. A harsh winter set in and many died. Seeing the Spaniards were not immortal, the Indians questioned if they were gods at all. They ordered them to heal their sick or they would stop bringing them food.

It is said that "Man's extremity is God's opportunity." If he were to survive, Cabeza de Vaca knew he must learn to be a faith healer and learn fast. He was naked, starving and totally helpless. In his book, LA RELACION, Cabeza de Vaca relates how, after fervent prayer, he was instructed by God how to heal the sick.

As time went by he made it to the mainland and became a trader. The various tribes might kill each other, but traders brought in welcomed goods and were given a pass.

He continued to make his way west where he knew he would eventually find a Spanish settlement. For a while he fell upon a tribe who enslaved him and three others of his original expedition. They were months in servitude before they made their escape.

As they walked west, the next tribe welcomed them. They had heard of their previous success as healers and took them to their sick. Hadn't Jesus healed the sick and said, "All these things I have done, you can do and more if you believe?" The Spainards had no choice. The Indians believed in their healing power and many were healed because of their belief. Cabeza de Vaca and his three companions continued on their way for hundreds of miles across Texas and beyond, barefoot and mostly naked. They had a large following as they progressed from tribe to tribe and news of their healing powers preceded them.

Texas has more churches than anyplace but has produced no recorded saints. We have seen more than our share of outlaws, law men, gamblers and drunks, but Cabeza de Vaca comes as close as any to being a holy man. He came to conquer and pillage, but ended up a healer and strong defender of the Native Americans.

After eight years, he and his companions met up with Spanish soldiers on the Sea of Cortez and made their way to Mexico City. Cabeza de Vaca sailed back to Spain where he spent three years writing of his adventures in a book titled, "LA RELACION."

I am forced to conclude that God made Texas on his day off, for pure entertainment, just to prove that all that diversity could be crammed into one section of earth by a really top hand.

Author Mary Lasswell

RENE-ROBERT CAVALIER,
SIEUR de LaSALLE (1643-1687)

A hundred and forty years after Cabeza de Vaca left Spain to colonize the Gulf coast, Rene-Robert Cavalier, Sieur de LaSalle set out from France for Canada. He was 23 years old and tried farming and fur trading before he got interested in expolration. Little was known about North America. LaSalle explored the Great Lakes and the Ohio River before he took a canoe trip down the Mississippi River in hopes it would prove to be a route to China.

Arriving at the Gulf Coast, he claimed the river and everything it drained for France. This was in 1682. The United States was obliged to buy much of it back in the Louisiana Purchase in 1803 for $11,250,000 and we still didn't know what we were buying. An expedition led by Louis and Clark went to find out.

After claiming all the real-estate drained by the Mississippi River, LaSalle went back to France and organized a group to set up a colony on the gulf Coast near the mouth of the Mississippi River. Four ships started out with 300 men, women, and children. One of the ships was taken by pirates in the West Indies before reaching the Gulf Coast.

So what does this have to do with Texas? Somehow LaSalle missed the Mississippi and ended up in Matagorda Bay in Texas where one of his remaining ships promptly broke up. Another went aground. The final ship sailed back to France. The population of the would-be colony dwindled down. They built Fort Saint Louis for protection from hostile Indians. LaSalle with 35 others left on foot searching for the Mississippi. They got somewhere in East Texas before LaSalle was murdered by one of his own men. His murderer was slain by the group who never returned to the fort but walked back to Canada. Months later natives killed all the adults at the fort and carried off five children who were never heard from again.

TEXAS UNDER SPANISH RULE

In 1519, Cortez with an army of only 600 conquered the Aztec Empire in Mexico. In 1532 Pizzaro with only 106 foot-soldiers and 62 horsemen killed the emperor of the vast Inca Empire and scattered his army of 80,000. The conquest stretched from present day Columbia all the way to the southern tip of South America.

The Spanish were capable conquistadors, but they were not able to subdue Texas. Three hundred years later in the early 1800's they still had only spotty outposts in Texas. The fierce horse Indians, the Comanche and Apache ruled the plains and raided settlements all the way to the Gulf Coast and across the Rio Grande River. Other tribes defended their territory as well. The vast Comancheria promised death to any settlers foolish enough to try to put down roots. Spain chose to open Texas to anyone brave enough to try to settle the place. The Spanish and later the newly independent Mexicans were tough, but they weren't tough enough for Texas. Though Spain claimed the territory we now call Texas, the native American Indians ruled it.

THE NUN IN BLUE

Senora (Sister) Maria Jesus de Agreda was a saintly young nun in a Franciscan Poor Clares convent in Agreda, Spain. In 1620, she had visions in which she was told to take the Christian message to the native peoples in the New World. In her devotions, she was transported there by bi-location while the physical body remained behind and the soul traveled. Over the next decade she made over 500 such journeys where she healed the sick, made converts, and instructed the natives of Jamano and Tejas tribes in the fundamentals of the faith. She was able to speak to them in their own tongue. She urged them to contact the Franciscan Friars on the Rio Grande near what is now Santa Fe, New Mexico.

On her journeys, she appeared in her usual dress of a course blue sackcloth cloak covering her nun's habit. She related tales of these journeys to those in her convent in Spain and news got out to Church officials. They in turn sent word to the new world to check out Sister Maria's stories.

The friars in New Mexico confirmed that indeed a delegation of some fifty Jamano Indians had requested the Franciscans to send missionaries. They had come from their homes somewhere far to the East in what is now Texas. They said they had been visited by a woman dressed in blue. They wanted to live as Christians.

The legend of the Lady in Blue continued to grow in the region long after her death. In the 1680's, the Spanish mounted an entrada into Texas. The intent was to tighten Spain's grip on empire and bring Christianity to the Indians. They also wanted to investigate the Indians' continuing stories about spiritual visits by the nun from Agreda, the Lady in Blue. Because of her role in prompting the early colonization of the state, Senora Maria has been regarded as the mother of Texas. In 1690, a quarter century after her death, a Tejas Indian chief in eastern Texas asked Damian Manzanet, a Franciscan missionary, for a piece of blue baize in which to bury his mother. He specified blue, the missionary said, because in times past the Tejas Indians had been visited by a beautiful woman, who came down from the heights, dressed in blue garments, and they wished to be like that woman.

MYSTERY WOMAN

Here is a true story involving a hermit, a cannibal, a naked lady, and pirates. This was back before Austin started his Texas colony. In about 1810 a man came to the mouth of the San Bernando River in what is now Texas. He was a hermit and his neighbors were the Karakawa Indians who had a nasty reputation for being cannibals. He made his peace with the Karankawas and they didn't bother him. The hermit befriended one young Karankawa lad and taught him to speak English.

Along came the hurricane of 1816. It is believed to be the strongest hurricane ever to hit the Texas coast, even worse than the 1900 storm that destroyed most of Galveston. The Indians who survived the storm did so by lashing themselves in the top of cedar trees to escape the storm surge. When the water receded, the English speaking Karankawa went in search of the hermit, but he had washed away. Instead he found a ship that had been carried inland by the storm. The crew was missing or dead, but he discovered a naked white woman wearing only a locket around her neck. She was chained by an ankle in the cabin till he freed her. She told him she was the daughter of a great white chief and the wife of a lesser chief. She said she had been on a great ship that had been attacked by pirates. Everyone aboard her ship had been killed but her. The priates had kept her as a love slave. The Karakawa took her as his wife, but she didn't live long. Before she died, she asked him to show the locket, engraved with the name Theodosia, to anyone who spoke English.

Later he served as interpreter for Stephen F. Austin who was setting up a colony. He was wearing the locket around his neck. When asked about it, he said that it had belonged to a white woman and told the story of how they had met, but no one knew who the lady had been talking about.

On December 25, 1813 the coasting Braque Patriot cleared Charleston harbor en route to New York. Aboard the Patriot was Mrs. Joseph Alliston, wife of South Carolina's Governor and her infant son. The boywas being taken to New York to meet his grandfather, Former United

States Vice President, Aaron Burr. The Patriot never reached New York, and its fate was unknown.

Some thirty years after the Patriot vanished, a drunken sailor dying in a Sailor's Home confessed he had been a crew member aboard the Patriot. As soon as the Patriot was out of sight of Charleston, he and other conspirators had taken over the ship, killed the passengers and crew and went pirating. The pirate trade persisted until the 1830's.

BRIT BALEY

It took a special breed to move to Texas in the early days. Brit Baley was a special breed. In 1821 he brought his family to Texas and squatted on land among hostile Indians. When Austin arrived in 1823, he told Brit he would have to move as he was on land designated by the Mexican government as part of the Austin Colony. Brit refused to move and there was no one brave enough to make him. He was a hard drinking, hot tempered eccentric, a fearless brawler who was not to be crossed.

In 1832, when Brit knew he was about to die of Cholera, he told his wife he wanted to be buried standing up and facing west where he had been ever moving all his life. So they dug a hole and dropped the coffin into it standing on end. He was buried with his rifle, two pistols, powder, and shot. Brit's servant, Uncle Bubba, added a jug of whiskey to send him on his way properly. However, his wife wouldn't have it. She took the whiskey and threw it out the window. It was the only time she was able to regulate Brit's whiskey. When you die, you lose your vote.

A strange eerie light was soon seen some nights on Brit's land. Bubba said it was his master who didn't rest easy without his whiskey. Ever since, there have been tales of Brit's ghost reappearing to roam his land. He first appeared in human form when another couple, Ann and Raney Thomas, bought the old Baley place. In 1836 on separate occasions, first Ann and later Raney, when sleeping in Baley's bedroom were awakened in the night experiencing cold and seeing the ghost of Baley moving about the room. It seems Brit is still searching for his whiskey. Strange appearances have occurred from time to time even as late as 1960 on the Baley place seven miles from Brazoria.

JOSIAH WILBARGER

In early August of 1833, Josiah Wilbarger joined four other men surveying land for settlement in pre-revolution Texas. They were attacked by fifty Comanche Indians. Two of the party ran to their horses and got away. Josiah and the other two were shot, stripped of their clothes, scalped and left for dead. Though the other two were dead, Josiah was still alive but in serious condition. He tried to crawl away, but was too weak to go far. After dark, he had a vision of his sister, Margaret Clifton, telling him to stay where he was. He would be rescued the following day.

Sarah Hornsby, wife of one of the men who had escaped, awoke from a dream and announced to her husband, that Josiah was not dead. She had seen him in her dream wounded but not dead. She saw him sitting naked, leaning against a tree. Her husband talked her into going back to sleep. Three hours later she had the same vivid dream. She got out of bed and at dawn had breakfast ready for the men in the house and insisted they go find Josiah. They protested saying they had seen him shot and scalped and that the Comanche never left a victim alive. Mrs. Hornsby would not be denied. Reluctantly they went to find Josiah.

Josiah was rescued and returned to the Hornsby house where Sarah nursed him back to health. He lived another dozen years. Sarah believed Josiah's sister must have brought her those dreams.

Six weeks after Josiah was rescued, a letter came advising Josiah that his sister, Margaret had died. At the time he had the vision of her, her body lay buried in the ground.

THE AUSTIN COLONY

Just as Mexico gained its independence from Spain, Stephen F. Austin obtained permission to organize a colony of 300 families in Texas. He wanted honest, hard-working people who would make the colony a success. A family of husband, wife and two children would receive 1,280 acres at twelve and a half cents per acre. By late 1825, Austin had brought the first 300 families to his settlement and obtained contracts to settle an additional 900 families.

One man was offered all of Galveston Island, but turned it down when he found the pelican eggs too salty.

Between 1825 and 1829, Austin exercised civil and military authority over the settlers. He introduced a semblance of American law and organized small armed groups to protect the colonists. These eventually evolved into the Texas Rangers.

MUSTANG

The Moors conquered Spain in AD 711 riding Arabian horses, a breed far superior to the European horses. When the Spanish at last were able to throw off the yoke of oppression in 1492, they kept one thing the Moors had brought, the Arabian horse. They crossed these with the European breeds to develop a superior horse for hunting and battle.

Cortez was the first to bring some of these horses to North America. Some got loose and went wild. By natural selection the hardiest thrived and evolved into the mustang. They changed the culture of the native plains Indians.

The word Mustang is derived from the Spanish meaning wild horse. They are known to be swift, surefooted, hardy, and intelligent with a lot of stamina.

The Native Americans were quick to take advantage of the Mustang. They had three hundred years to develop a culture surrounding the horse for hunting and warfare by the time Anglos began to settle Texas. No horse was better suited to the Comanche than these Mustangs. The mustang could forage up to fifty miles from water. They could thrive on sparse grass and had tremendous endurance. The Anglos came with their less adaptable mounts. When the white man offered horses to the Indians, the Indians were quick to neuter them so as not to compromise their stock.

Early Anglo Texans might use the Mustang as their symbol. They were once domesticated, but when they moved to Texas, the harsh environment weeded out the weak and strengthened those who endured.

AN EARLY RODEO

Texas Rangers were hired to protect the settlers in Texas but on at least one occasion in 1834, Comanche and Texas Rangers squared off in San Antonio for a rodeo of sorts to see who the best horsemen were. Town residents came out to watch and someone described the event.

The Rangers wore buckskins and slouched hats, and sported pistols and knives in their belts. Before the event a few of them retreated, horses and all, into a barroom for drinks.

The Comanche in feathers, furs, and painted faces sat confidently on their mounts. From early childhood, they were trained to fight from astride their mustang ponies.

Mexican caballeros rode proudly to the field wearing big sombreros, bright scarves, and colorful trousers.

The events started with each rider—at full gallop—retrieving a spear from flat on the ground. The Indians used no saddle or stirrups. It is hard to imagine how they managed to pick anything off the ground from a running horse.

Then a target was put down. The Indians shot two arrows at full gallop into the target, Rangers and Caballeros a like number of bullets. The pistols were muzzle loaders. It would take two pistols. One could not ride and reload a pistol at the same time. Trick riding techniques and modes of attack and defense followed. Horse breaking concluded the competition.

A young man from Florida won first place. The Indians took the remaining honors.

San Antonio was a rough place, the most westward pioneer settlement in Texas.

JAMES BOWIE

The Texas history we learned in school told about Jim Bowie and his famous knife, I never heard why it was so famous. Why didn't he just carry a gun like everyone else? Here is the story.

Bowie had a feud going with Sheriff Norris Wright in Mississippi from when he supported Wright's opponent in the race for sheriff. Wright, a bank director, had then turned down a Bowie loan application. After a confrontation on the street one day, Wright fired a shot at Bowie. Bowie attempted to return fire, but his pistol misfired. Then he tried to kill Wright with his bare hands. He was big enough to do it. Wright's friends stopped the attack. Fire arms in that day were unreliable muzzle loaders. One shot and it took a while to reload. After that set-to with Wright, Bowie always carried a larege knife to back up his pistol.

The following year, Bowie and Wright, along with other seconds and onlookers attended a duel on a sandbar outside of Natchez, Mississippi. The duelists each fired twice and missed then shook hands. Honor had been served. Other members present, however, disliked each other and began fighting. Bowie was shot in the hip. He fired his pistol but the fight was just beginning. He drew his knife and charged his attacker, who hit Bowie over the head with his empty pistol knocking Bowie to the ground. Wright shot at and missed the prone Bowie. The then drew his sword cane and impaled Bowie to the ground. When he attempted to retrieve his blade by placing his foot on Bowie's chest and tugging, Bowie pulled him down and disemboweled him with his knife.

Newspapers ran the story of the Sandbar Fight describing Bowie's fighting prowess and his knife. Bowie did not start the fight. He just finished it. Then others saw the wisdom of carrying a knife to back up their pistol. People called these knives Bowie knives and knife makers as far away as Europe were producing them and sending them to America.

In 1828, after recovering from wounds suffered in the sandbar fight, Bowie moved to Texas. On the way, he stopped off in Washington, Arkansas and had the blacksmith make him a knife that is now known as "THE BOWIE KNIFE." It was formidable weapon and with Bowie's size and reputation, he needed only to open his jacket and reveal the knife to discourage anyone who might want to challenge him. Newspaper accounts had made him world famous.

If you care to own a knife like Bowie's you can stop by Washington, Arkansas today and have the current black smith make you one with special steel, tempered to perfection and a custom grip fitted to your hand. He is proud of his knives. He will make you one for a thousand dollars. On the other hand you might buy a modern day multi-shot pistol. They are much more reliable these days and you don't have to get so up-close to make your point.

The Constitution of Mexico banned religions other than Roman Catholicism. Bowie was baptized into the Roman Catholic faith. On February 20, he took an oath of allegiance to Mexico and his fluency in Spanish helped him establish himself in San Antonio. He was elected a commander, with the rank of colonel, of the Texas Rangers later that year.

Bowie became a Mexican citizen on September 30, 1830, giving him the right to buy up to 11 leagues of public land. In addition, he convinced 14 other citizens to apply for land in order to turn it over to him, giving him 700,000 acres for speculation.

On April 25, 1831, Bowie married 19-year-old Maria Ursula de Veramendi, the daughter of his business partner and vice governor of the province. At the time, Bowie claimed to have a net worth of $223, 000 (44,580,000 today) although it was mostly in land value. He and his bride moved into the Veramendi Palace, living with Ursula's parents. He appeared to have a bright future but the battle of the Alamo lay in his future instead.

SEEDS OF REBELLION

At first, the Mexican government encouraged immigration so settlers could defend themselves against Indian raids. By 1833 there were 30,000 Anglos (people whose primary language is English) in Texas, 5,000 slaves, and only 7,800 Mexican born. The American settlers found their rights under the Mexican dictatorship were not what they enjoyed back home. Fearing a secession movement, dictator, Santa Anna, forbade any further immigration from the United States. Settlers learned they could no longer grow cotton, the best cash crop, but must grow corn and other crops as dictated by the government., nor could they own slaves. They must tithe to the Catholic Church. Promised tax exemptions were rescinded. Tariffs increased on goods from the United States. Mexican troops in Texas were largely criminals who were given the choice of serving in Texas or going to jail. The new laws didn't set well with the Texans. Besides, they wanted their own separate state. The current capitol was in Saltillo, 400 miles to the south. They sent Austin to Mexico City to petition Santa Anna, but Santa Anna refused. When Austin sent word back to Texas, he suggested Texas independence might be an alternative. The message was intercepted and Austin was jailed.

In early 1835 immigration from the U.S. Increased dramatically in spite of the restriction. Santa Anna believed it was a plot. He jailed cotton farmers, dissolved state legislatures, and disbanded militias. When the Mexican government demanded a cannon supplied to the militia in Gonzales be returned, the Texans refused, saying, "Come and take it." Then eighteen Texans held off a hundred Mexican troops who came for it. By December, armed Texans, in a series of conflicts had run off all organized Mexican garrisons in Texas.

COME AND TAKE IT

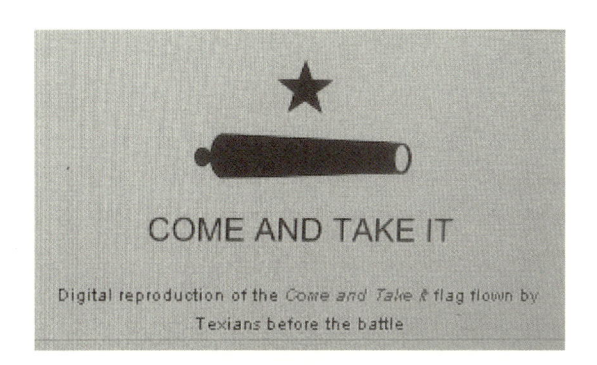

Digital reproduction of the *Come and Take It* flag flown by Texians before the battle

I must say as to what I have seen of Texas, it is the garden spot of the world, the best land and the best prospects for health I ever saw, and I do believe it is a fortune to any man to come here.

Alamo hero Davy Crockett

THE TEXAS REVOLUTION

To quell the rebellion, Santa Anna assembled an army of 6,000 and marched to Texas. It was February second before he crossed the Rio Grande. On February 23, 1836, 1500 Mexican soldiers entered San Antonio. They surrounded the Alamo where some 186 determined Texans had taken a stand.

Colonel James W. Fannin

THE GOLIAD MASSACRE

When the Mexican army crossed the Rio Grande, Santa Anna headed for San Antonio and the Alamo while Mexican General Jose Urea with some 900 troops, split off and followed a coastal route into Texas.

At San Patricio, Urea encountered 50 Texans. Frank Johnson and four of his men escaped, but the rest were either killed or captured. Later, the Mexicans came across another 50 men, and killed all but one.

Refugio was the next town in Urea's path. James W. Fannin, commander of the garrison at Goliad, sent two relief forces. The first numbered thirty men, followed by a larger group of some 50 men. Like Johnson's bunch, Urea's army killed or captured both of these groups.

Back in Goliad, Fannin and his remaining 350 men were ordered to aid William Barrett Travis at the Alamo. Due to indecision and carelessness Fannin, failed to act promptly.

Five days after receiving the order, Fannin began his march and soon found himself surrounded on an open prairie by the Mexican army. Heavily outnumbered, the Texans waved the white flag of truce, believing they would be taken captive and eventually returned to their homes, the Texans surrendered the morning of March 20. They were escorted back to Goliad as prisoners.

When news of their capture reached Santa Anna, he was furious that the Texans had not been executed on the spot. Citing his recently passed law that all foreigners taken under arms would be treated as pirates and executed, Santa Anna sent orders to execute the Goliad prisoners.

On Palm Sunday, March 27, the prisoners were divided into three groups, marched onto open prairie, and shot. All of Fannin's command except a few that managed to escape were massacred, collected into piles, and burned.

PRESIDIO LA BAHIA

Presidio La Bahia, the fort where Fannin and his troops were garrisoned at the beginning of the Texas revolution is the most fought over fort in Texas history. It participated in six National wars for independence.

In 1721 the Spanish built it on what was left of La Salle's Fort St. Louis on Lavaca Bay. In 1726 it was rebuilt near Victoria. In 1749 it was relocated to Goliad.

By 1810 Goliad was the second largest town in Spanish Texas.

During the American Revolution, soldiers from the Presidio assisted the Spanish army fighting the British along the Gulf Coast. Thus Goliad was one of the only towns west of the Mississippi River to participate in the American Revolution.

In a lead up to the Texas Revolution, a bunch of Texans on October 9, 1835 routed the Mexican troops occupying the Presidio. The first Texas Declaration of Independence was printed there in December 1835 and distributed throughout Texas. When the Mexican army came there in March of 1836, twice as many Texans died than at the Alamo.

The chapel at the Presidio has seen continuous use since the 1700s. It is one of the oldest churches in America.

THE BATTLE OF THE ALAMO

January 9, 1836, after losing his bid for a fourth term as a Tennessee representative to the U.S. Congress, Davy Crockett wrote a letter stating his intention to go to Texas. This, his last letter, praises Texas as, "the garden spot of the world," with the "best land and the best prospects for health I ever saw." With high optimism for his political future, he wrote that he fully expected to take part in writing a constitution for Texas. "I am in hopes," he wrote, "of making a fortune yet for myself and my family, bad as my prospect has been." Crockett did not foresee his fate at the battle of the Alamo, which occurred just two months later.

On March 5, 1836, 26 year old Colonel William Travis assembled the 186 men in the courtyard of the Alamo. Santa Anna's army had laid siege for a dozen days, constantly bombarding the old mission. The situation was hopeless. It was obvious neither reinforcements nor supplies would be coming.

William B. Travis became sole Texian commander at the Alamo on February 24.

"Colonel Travis drew his sword, placed the tip in the ground and drew a line in front of the assembled men. He stood on one side of the line facing the rest of the defenders on the other side. It was a solemn moment.

He declared that he would stay and defend the garrison. It was his duty for as long as he drew breath. He then told the others if they wished to join him they could step over the line. If not, they were free to leave any way they thought they could.

"I'd like to ask each of you what it is you value so highly that you are willing to fight and possibly die for. We will call that Texas. The Mexican army hopes to lure us into attempting escape. Almost anything seems better than remaining in this place, penned up. If, however, we force the enemy to attack, I believe every one of you will prove himself worth ten in return. We will not only show the world what patriots are made of, but we will also deal a crippling blow to the army of Santa Anna."

The men began stepping across the line by twos and threes. They all did with the exception of Louis (Moses) Rose and Colonel Bowie who was dying and lay on a makeshift stretcher. He asked someone, anyone, to carry him across the line.

"I don't deserve mercy, said Bowie. "I do deserve a drink. You got anything stronger than water?"

Only Rose failed to accept the challenge. He managed to make his escape under the cover of darkness. Though he lived for another twelve years, he was despised as a deserter wherever he went.

Soon after the line in the sand, Santa Anna ordered a final assault. All Alamo defenders lost their lives. 400 to 600 Mexican fighters died. A third of the Mexicans were either killed or wounded.

HOUSTON TAKES COMMAND

While Santa Anna engaged the Alamo, Texas leaders met at Washington on the Brazos to formerly declare Texas independence and form a government. Sam Houston was officially appointed Commander in Chief of the armed forces. Unfortunately he had no armed forces to command.

After the battle at the Alamo, Santa Anna split his forces and with 700 soldiers marched toward Galveston hoping to capture members of the newly formed Texas Provisional Government.

Sam Houston, meanwhile, scraped together a rag-tag group of 900 patriots eager to defend Texas and make the Declaration of Independence stick.

Santa Anna chased Houston's small force across Texas. The Texans began to grumble, "Are we never going to stop and fight?" Some even dropped out in disgust.

Sam Houston responded, "In 1815, Napoleon escaped from Elba. He moved swiftly to consolidate before the Grand Alliance could move against him. Wellington, with fewer men, retreated ahead of Napoleon, forcing Napoleon to chase him through Belgium. Wellington had a vision of a battlefield. He did not know where it was, but he knew he would know it when he saw it. He continued moving, waiting for that ground and for Napoleon to make a mistake. Gentlemen, I do not consider myself to be Wellington' Santa Anna, however, considers himself to be Napoleon – the Napoleon of the West. I will continue to retreat gentlemen, until I find the ground in my vision and, when Santa Anna makes his mistake, I will attack."

On April 20, the two armies met at the San Jacinto River. Mexican General Cos arrived with an additional 450 men, swelling Santa Anna's army to over 1,200. Santa Anna was delighted to finally engage the last trace of Texas resistance. Confident that the Texans would not attempt to challenge his superior numbers, he ordered his army to stand down and rest up before the final dispatch of Houston's rabble. Tomorrow would be time enough for that. That was his mistake. He was so confident he didn't even post lookouts. That was a bigger mistake.

About 3:30 in the afternoon, while the Mexicans were enjoying their siesta, the Texans attacked. The battle lasted less than twenty minutes and Santa Anna's entire force was either killed or captured. Nine Texans died.

Santa Anna escaped the turmoil of battle but was captured the following day. Most of the Texans wanted to execute him on the spot remembering Santa Anna's policy of taking no prisoners, but Houston played it better. He offered to spare Santa Anna's life if he would order the rest of his army back to Mexico and sign a peace treaty ceding all claim to Texas. In order to save his own life, Santa Anna complied.

This was heady stuff for Texans who had won against the 6,000 man Mexican army that first arrived in Texas.

Texas was a sovereign nation with its own currency and navy. Later, when Texas became a state, a mindset persisted among the population that Texans were not like other Americans, but somehow a bit better. When they built their capitol building, they made sure the dome was taller than the capital dome in Washington. When they built a victory monument at San Jacinto similar to the Washington monument in DC, they topped it with the lone Texas star and built it a little taller than the Washington monument.

Texans to this day tend to take on an attitude of swagger that the rest of Americans find insufferable. Texas is recognized around the world as being different, as well it should. After all, it is Texas. John Wayne wasn't born in Texas, but he knew how to act like a Texan. Real men aspire to be like John Wayne.

Texas is the finest portion of the globe that has blessed my vision.

Sam Houston

THE YELLOW ROSE OF TEXAS

She was twenty years old and born of mixed race, not quite white and not quite black, a kind of high yellow and pretty. Born Emily West, but when Colonel James Morgan bought her, she took on the name of Emily Morgan. He brought her to Texas in 1835, where it was against the law to own slaves; her status was officially changed to indentured servant with a 99 year term.

Colonel Morgan was in Galveston when General Santa Anna marched through with his army. Santa Anna took a shine to pretty Emily and took her with him to San Jacinto where he planned to decimate Houston's forces. He had them outnumbered and considered them a rag-tag bunch of undisciplined farmers worthy only of disdain. He had them cornered now. They were surrounded by water and could not escape. He would take them on tomorrow at his leisure.

He set up his elaborate three room tent equipped with cases of champagne and bed with silk sheets. Tomorrow he would deal with Houston. Today he would rest and let Emily entertain him. Entertain him she did, distracting him in the most delightful ways. He was so distracted he was not even dressed when the Texans charged into camp. Santa Anna was barely able to leap on his horse and escape only to be captured the following day.

Emily Morgan's service at San Jacinto was without equal. She kept Santa occupied which facilitated the victory that gave birth to the Republic of Texas. The battle at San Jacinto eventually brought Texas into the United States, and later added the future states of New Mexico, Arizona, California, Utah, Colorado, Wyoming, Kansas and Oklahoma. This doubled the size of the United States and gave us "America from sea to shining sea." If one were to calculate total real-estate value against the hours of service, one would have to conclude she was the most valuable call girl in all history.

To this day, we sing her song here in Texas.

"She's the sweetest little rose-bud that Texas ever knew. Her eyes are bright as diamonds, they sparkle like the dew. You may talk about your Clementine and sing of Rose-a-lee, but the yellow rose of Texas is the only girl for me."

TEXAS NAVIES

In 1836 when Texas proclaimed its independence from Mexico, Texas faced invasion, on land and sea by overwhelming forces. Mexico had many times the military resources of the new Republic. Texas triumphed over the superiorly equipped enemy at San Jacinto. One of the most important elements of that victory was the determined maritime activity of the Texas Navy.

The Texas fleet amounted to four small sailing ships that prevented the Mexicans from sending a second army to trap General Sam Houston and his small command between two immensely superior forces. During a series of raids in the Gulf of Mexico, the Texas ships INDEPENDENCE, BRUTUS, INVINCIBLE, and LIBERTY kept the Mexican coastal towns in fear and forced the enemy navy to disperse its strength in order to protect its property and shipping. The Texans thus prevented Mexican ships from supplying Santa Anna. In the process, they captured arms to supply Houston's army to win the victory at San Jacinto. After that vital triumph, the Texas Navy was disbanded.

Mexico refused to acknowledge Texas' independence. In 1839 it began to assemble a much larger force against the Texas Republic. The Texas Congress supplied vessels and established the Second Texas Navy. The new Navy constantly scrambled for supplies and was often maintained by personal credit of the commander and Secretary of the Navy, S. Rhodes Fisher and by the capture of Mexican ships and cargoes. The Texans repeated the tactics of the former Texas Navy.

For three years, the Second Texas Navy pummeled the Mexican coast from the Rio Grande to Yucatan and engaged the Mexican fleet. The Texans raided and burned Mexican cities and shipping and made reckless attacks without considering odds or size of Mexican ships.

Off Yucatan, a Texas sailing ship engaged and defeated a Mexican war steamer, a unique victory in the annals of naval history. The invasion plans were scrubbed because Mexico was too harassed by the exploits of Texas sailors. The Texas Navy secured the continued sovereignty of the Republic on the high seas until Texas joined the United States in 1845 when the Texas fleet was absorbed by the United States Navy.

THE REPUBLIC OF TEXAS OPEN FOR BUSINESS

Sam Houston was elected the first President of the Republic of Texas. Being the hero of the day, he defeated Stephen Austin for the office. Realizing that Texas needed to join the United States for protection against another invading Mexican army, he ran on that platform and the population agreed. Texas didn't have the troops to protect its new border with Mexico. Fortunately for Texas, Mexico never mounted another large invasion. Texas was not able to defend itself and the United States was not yet interested in annexing Texas.

Houston was given the keys to the executive mansion.

The executive mansion at Houston
Courtesy Harris County Heritage Society

It was a two room shack with a dirt floor that he shared with another guy in what is now the city of Houston.

Two years later when Mirabeau B. Lamar was elected to replace him he moved the capitol to the location of present day Austin because of all the mud, cholera and yellow fever in the original capitol. Sam Houston and Lamar didn't like each other. Houston dressed in his finest to attend

Lamar's inauguration. He was scheduled to say a few words before Lamar's inaugural address. Instead, Houston gave an oration that went on for hours so there wasn't time for Lamar to give his speech.

In 1841 Lamar sent troops to take what is now Santa Fe, New Mexico. The venture was ill conceived and the Mexicans captured them without firing a shot.

On September 11, 1842, a thousand Mexican troops seized control of San Antonio for a short time. It was plain to see, Texas was not sufficiently strong to retain its independence. They would eventually either be forced back under Mexican control or join the United States.

The United States under President Tyler was more open to annexing Texas. On December 29, 1845, Texas became the 28th state.

THE GREAT RAID OF 1840

Just because the Texans defeated Santa Anna in the spring of 1836 didn't mean Texas would see peace. There were skirmishes on land and sea with the Mexicans wanting to take back their territory.

An equal problem was the Comanche Indians who still considered the land was theirs. These Comanche were better horsemen than the U.S. Calvary. A settler had his musket, but if he missed on the first shot, a Comanche could pump six arrows into him while he reloaded. The Indians had successfully fended off the Spanish for over three hundred years. That is why the Anglos were invited to settle in the first place.

The Comanche didn't care much for farming, preferring instead to raid those who farmed. They would swoop in on a homestead, kill the men, rape the women, and take off with anything they wanted including children to raise as their own or keep for slaves, yet the settlers kept pouring in to Texas anyway.

Four years after the war of Texas independence, the Comanche decided to sue for peace. They wanted lasting recognition of their homeland, the Comancheria to be off limits to whites. The Comancheria encompassed a large part of Texas, Oklahoma and some of New Mexico.

The Texans wanted to settle the Comancheria and the Comanche to return captured whites. Neither side was willing to cede to the other's demands.

The Indians were assured safe passage to meet on March 13, 1840 at the council house in San Antonio. They were betrayed by the Texans who ambushed them, killing all the 33 chiefs and twenty four of their wives and children. Rightly so, the Comanche soon launched the great raid of 1840 in retaliation.

The Indian and the white man's cultures could never mix. One must wipe out the other. Following the Council House slaughter of his people, Comanche War Chief, Buffalo Hump, sought revenge. He spread the word to all Comanche that he was raiding white settlements. 400 warriors, the largest raiding party ever assembled, gathered. Wives and young boys went along to do the work. There were as many as a thousand Comanche who set out to raid the towns of Victoria and Linnville. They attacked Victoria before the citizens could be warned. Townspeople hid in their houses and shops. After killing a dozen or so people the Indians departed Victoria and headed for the coast.

On August 7, 1840, the Indians surrounded Linnville, the second largest port in the Republic of Texas, then pillaged the stores and houses. Linnville, now a ghost town, was just outside of present day Port Lavaca. The citizens fled to the safety of the water. They boarded small boats and a schooner anchored in the bay and watched the destruction of their town. All day the Comanche looted and burned buildings. They clad themselves in plundered hats and clothes, tied feather beds and bolts of cloth to their horses, then herded cattle into pens and slaughtered them. One outraged citizen grabbed a gun and waded ashore and roared at the warriors, but the Indians spared him, believing him mad. He later found he had waded ashore to face nearly a thousand Indians with an unloaded pistol. Maybe he was mad.

A total inventory of over $300,000 in goods was reported to be at Linnville including silver bullion in addition to other trade goods. The Indians went wild over several cases of hats and umbrellas. These they grabbed and strutted about the burning town playing dress up. On the afternoon of August 8, they loaded their prizes on pack mules and departed.

The Rangers had been trailing the war party for some time, unable to engage them because of their sheer numbers. But the two days of looting at Linnville gave the militia and Ranger companies a chance to gather. Volunteers from Gonzales and Bastrop with all the ranger companies of east and central Texas moved to intercept the Indians. They made contact at Plum Creek, near the city of Lockhart on August 12. The usual Comanche tactic was to raid as fast as possible then flee from the scene of a victory, but on this occasion they slowed to a gentler pace acceptable to the heavily laden pack mules. The militia and rangers caught the raiders, which normally would have been impossible. The battle of Plum Creek was a running skirmish, where the Texans tried to kill the raiders and recover loot, and the Indians attempted to get away. The Texans reported killing 80 Comanche. But greed saved the Comanche. When the militia discovered the stolen bullion, they abandoned the fight, divided their loot, and went home.

TEXAS RANGERS

Settlers coming into Texas in 1823 were met by fierce Comanche Indians on horseback who raided homesteads and were gone before any organized military defense could be mounted. Stephen F. Austin organized the first unit of the Texas Rangers consisting of ten men. He paid them fifty cents a day payable in land. Considering the vast area to protect, it was obvious the Rangers must be on horseback. Each ranger supplied his own horse and fire arms. All the government supplied was ammunition. Over the years Ranger units formed to meet some specific challenge, and were then disbanded due to the limited resources of the government. It seemed too little to make a difference, but without the Rangers, settlement of Texas would have been abandoned. Ranger leaders were selected among themselves. The odds were stacked in the Comanche's favor. It tends to explain why the Texas Rangers developed into such a lean, mean fighting force. They had to be innovative to survive.

In the 1836 revolution, faced by the armies of Santa Anna, the Ranger Companies became a part of the insurgent Texas army. They rode between retreating Texas forced and advancing Mexicans, serving as a rear guard and helping civilians clear out ahead of the enemy.

After the republic was established, sporadic but serious conflict between Texas and Mexico continued. Now the Rangers faced two enemies—Indians and Mexican troops. For more than a dozen years, they operated as irregular fighting units, serving as scouts, guerrillas, and cavalry support for regular soldiers, particularly between the Nueces and the Rio Grande. They also patrolled the ambiguous northwestern frontier in frequent battle with the Indians.

In the Mexican War Rangers enlisted as units of the United States Army. At war's end they returned to a dual role, protecting the western frontier and acting as guards on the newly established southern border of the United States, the Rio Grande. They built a reputation for quick striking power over a vast area, often with few riders. To the Anglo-American settler and businessman, the Ranger stood for courage, peacekeeping, and frontier resourcefulness. To his opponents, he represented the use of unhesitating violence and unrelenting pursuit.

Rangers were the peace officers, a state police force. They put down cattle rustling, fence cutting, mob violence...any breach of the law too violent or wide spread for local police.

An interesting group of Rangers in the early days of the republic was a unit under Isaac W. Burton which earned the title of "Horse marines." Burton, a Ranger captain since 1835, was given the job of patrolling the Texas coast in 1836 after the battle of San Jacinto. Mexico by no means recognized the Republic of Texas so the Texans feared a Mexican landing by sea.

The Rangers sighted a vessel June 3 in Copano Bay and Burton's men concealed themselves while one signaled the ship. A number of Mexican sailors rowed ashore in a small boat and were quickly captured. Sixteen Rangers then took the boat and rowed back out. Apparently mistaken at first for friends, they captured the *WATCHMAN* lying offshore with supplies for the Mexican army. But before the Rangers could leave the bay with the captured vessel, two other Mexican ships, the *COMANCHE* and *FANNY BUTLER* sailed in.

The Rangers forced the captain of the WATCHMAN to decoy the officers of the other two ships aboard. They captured them and soon were in command of all three ships, loaded with a net haul of $25,000 in supplies. These were turned over to the regular Texas army at Velasco, ending one of the few amphibious operations of the Texas Rangers.

Texas Ranger Captain L. H. McNelly

TEXAS RANGER CAPTAIN L. H. MCNELLY

In 1875 the Texas governor directed Ranger Captain L.H. McNelly to organize a company of Rangers to clean out the lawlessness in the Nueces strip, the land between the Nueces and Rio Grande rivers. Over 700,000 cattle had been rustled by Mexican bandits. In addition, armed bands of local citizens of Corpus Christi were killing innocent Mexicans. The strip had a reputation as a gathering place for outlaws.

It took only two days for McNelly to recruit forty men. They were mostly young men who had come to Texas because they were wanted by the law elsewhere.

Rangers were the law. It was generally not feasible to bring criminals vast distances to be tried. A horse thief was hanged on the spot where he was caught.

One of McNelly's riders was Casus Sandoval, a Mexican who took great pleasure in torturing Mexicans. Mexican bandits had burned down his home, killed his livestock and raped his wife and daughter while he was away. Sandoval had gone into frenzy, crossing into Mexico and killing fifty Mexican bandits before joining McNelly. Since he enjoyed it so much, Sandoval was the company executioner.

McNelly was only five foot six inches tall and weighed a hundred and thirty five pounds. He was suffering from tuberculosis, but his courage, iron will, and daring set the standard for all rangers who came after. He inspired fierce loyalty in his men. He would sometimes have to take leave and be nursed back to health by his wife.

Early on, McNelly made a daring raid into Mexico to confront a stronghold of rustlers. When he met armed Mexicans on horseback of much greater force, he was obliged to retreat to the Rio Grande. The Mexicans offered to give him safe passage across the river back into Texas and they would return the stolen cattle the next day. He seemed in no position to argue, but instead, he demanded the cattle right then and the bandits who took them. That is the way McNelly was. He would not back down. The raids into Mexico created an international incident. National boundaries didn't impress him. He was only interested in getting the job done.

Later he captured famous outlaw John Fisher plus 800 cattle that Fisher had rustled. He took Fisher and his band to Eagle Pass and turned them over to the Sheriff. It was the first time he had taken prisoners. The Sheriff allowed there was no current warrant out for Fisher's arrest and Fisher's lawyer demanded that McNelly show witnesses to the crimes that everyone knew Fisher had committed. MnNelly had to give Fisher back his guns and let him go.

Times were changing in Texas. The lawyers were taking over and Rangers had to change their ways. With McNelly's invasion of Mexico and Fisher's false arrest, he had become an embarrassment to the Governor. His Rangers were disbanded and McNelly was put out to pasture. He was too weak to farm and soon died of his illness, leaving wife and children to fend for themselves. There was no pension. The three dollars a day he had made as Ranger Captain was all spent.

1840 FRONTIER

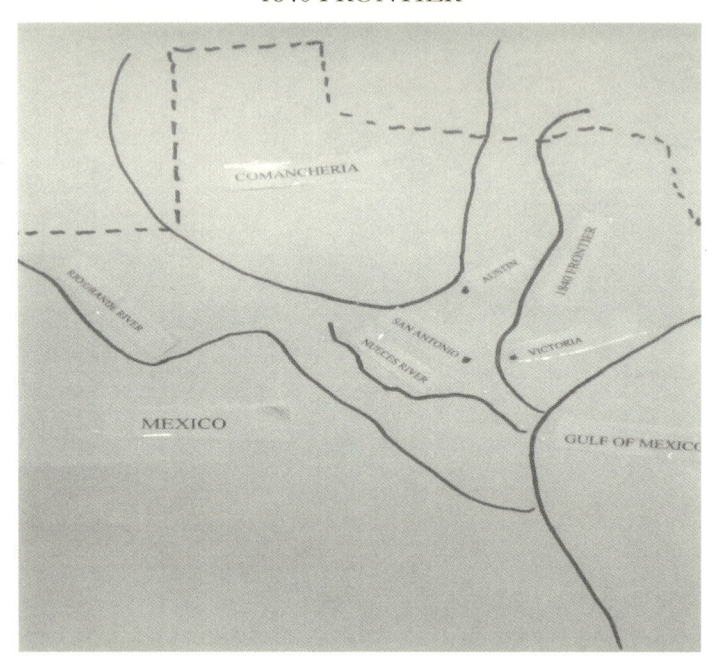

Here is a crude drawing of what Texas looked like in 1840. Note the small portion to the right of the 1840 frontier line was all that had substantial control by the settlers and even that was subject to raids by the Indians. San Antonio and Austin were still in Indian Territory. The dotted line showing the border was not a boundary for the new republic of Texas. It is drawn in here so the reader can get a better handle as it would be in present day Texas.

RANGER ALEXANDER WALLACE

Here is oversized Ranger William Alexander Wallace. He was descended from the famous family of William Wallace of Scottish fame and also Robert Bruce. Returning alone from a scout, he once emerged from a thicket and found himself face to face with 30 Comanche braves. It appeared he was surely a dead man. But Wallace yelled over his shoulder, "Come on boys, here they are!" The Indians scattered and Wallace made it back to camp.

By January of 1836, Ranger pay had increased to $25 a month.

Another story of the type all too common in those days, a woman was traveling with her husband, brother and two children when a band of Indians attacked. They killed the men and one child and captured the woman and her baby. After traveling some distance, they bedded down in a cedar thicket on the Colorado River near where present day Austin is today. The woman escaped without her baby and spent all night wading through the icy water. She arrived at a Ranger camp by mid-afternoon the next day. The Rangers broke camp immediately, tracked down the Indians, rescued the baby and killed one of the Indians before the rest fled.

"One riot, one ranger," is a phrase made famous by Teas Ranger Captain W.J. McDonald in the very early 1900's. McDonald was called upon by a Dallas mayor to stop an illegal Prize-fight and ease an angry mob. When stepping off the train, he was asked, "Where are the others?" To that McDonald replied, "Hell, ain't I enough? There's only one riot."

JACK HAYS, TEXAS RANGER

In 1844 problems with Comanche raids and the threat of invasion from Mexico made it necessary to defend the western and southwestern frontiers. Texas turned to a notable young Ranger commander, John Coffee Hays.

Hays established himself as a natural leader whom grizzled veterans would follow to their deaths if asked. Hays and his men saved the Republic of Texas on more than one occasion and rescued the U.S. Army in the coming war with Mexico.

He formed the Texas Rangers into an unorthodox, highly effective "special force" capable of moving fast and operating behind enemy lines. He incorporated Indian guerrilla tactics, adopted centuries-old Hispanic styles of frontier horsemanship, and introduced new technology such as Colt's five-shot revolver and revolving rifle. For years the Rangers had been armed with muzzle loading muskets and pistols. They developed the tactic of dismounting from their horses when confronted by Indians and half the Rangers firing. Then while the first half was reloading, the other half would fire their weapons. If the Indians could draw the fire of all the Rangers, they could attack with impunity while all the Rangers were reloading.

The Texas Navy was equipped with Colt five-shot revolvers but Texas was so strapped for funds they disbanded the Navy and gave the new pistols to the Rangers. On June 8th, 1844, the Rangers engaged in an event that would later result in the birth of the "Colt's Patent Firearms Company." Ranger Captain Jack Coffee Hays and a company of fourteen Rangers were returning to San Antonio after a patrol when they were attacked near the Pedernales River by a mounted force of 80 Comanche Indians. The Rangers immediately counter-attacked the Indians with their new Colt pistols. When the battle was over, the Comanche fled leaving more than half of their warriors behind,dead. Word of the Rangers great victory over the Comanche soon spread. For their part, the Rangers attributed their very survival to the firepower provided by the Colt revolver. The Comanche no longer had the advantage in battle. The Indians called Hays, "Devil Hays."

One of the Rangers, who participated in "Hays' big fight" as it was called, was Samuel Walker. When the U.S. Entered into war with Mexico in 1846, Walker joined a unit named the "U.S. Mounted Rifle Regiment." Walker convinced his superiors of the value of the revolver and was subsequently assigned to contact Samuel Colt and arrange for the delivery of new revolvers. Walker went to Colt and together they designed the pistol that became as the Walker Colt.

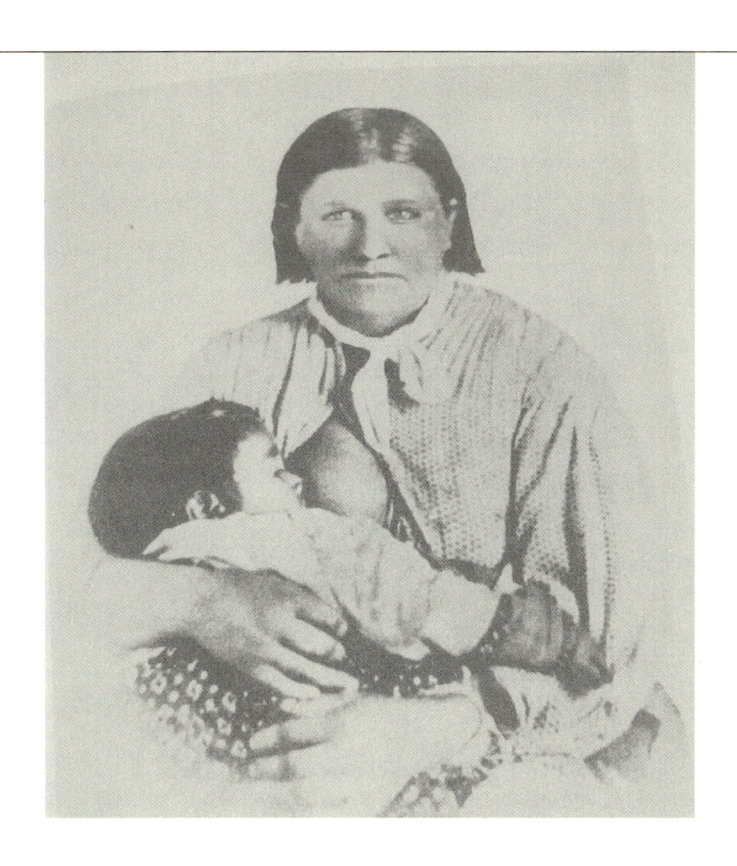

CYNTHIA ANN PARKER

Not long after the battle of San Jacinto, a band of five hundred Comanche and Kiowa Indians raided Fort Parker near present day Groesbeck, Texas. They killed the men and carried off some women and children; among them was nine year old Cynthia Ann Parker.

In her teens, Cynthia Ann married a Comanche war chief and had three of his children. The oldest was a boy, Quanah, born when Cynthia Ann was twenty.

After living with the Comanche for twenty five years, she was "rescued" by a large band of Rangers, soldiers, and cowboys in 1860. For Cynthia Ann, it was more like abduction. She had her young daughter with her, but she would never see her sons or husband again. She could not speak

English. After being returned to her original Parker family, she tried to escape several times to search for her children, but was caught and returned to relatives. Her daughter soon died and Cynthia Ann spent her final days grieving for the loss of her husband and children.

Quanah Parker, last of the Comanche Chiefs

The days of the Indians running free in Texas were coming to a close. White men killed the buffalo and forced the Indians into a reservation at Fort Sill in Oklahoma. The last holdout was Chief Quanah. On June 2, 1875, Quanah led his band of 400 warriors and 2,000 ponies to Fort Sill.

Quanah soon became the spokesman for all the Comanche on the Reservation. He also served with two other men as judge over Indians breaking the law.

The cattle drives were on and the Indians were charging a dollar a head for cows crossing reservation land. Indians also charged grazing rights on their land. Quanah himself owned 44,000 acres and became rich leasing it for grazing. He had a large two story white house built with separate bedrooms for his three wives. H was a major stock holder in the Acme and Pacific Rail Road and made trips to Washington to promote Indian interests. He adopted the Parker name and wore a dapper suit with black felt derby when visiting Dallas, Ft. Worth or Washington. He was the last and greatest of the free Comanche chiefs.

GERONIMO

Geronimo, Chiricahua Apache leader

It wasn't just the Comanche early Texans had to deal with. The Apaches were a force to be reckoned with. They resented the encroachment of Mexicans into traditional Apache territory. The Mexicans didn't seem to get it. Hadn't Spain claimed the whole western Hemisphere a long time ago and Mexico took it from Spain?

Between 1820 and the time of the Texas Revolution some 5,000 Mexicans died in Apache raids and 100 settlements were destroyed. Mexico placed a bounty on Apache scalps.

In 1858, when he was 29, four hundred Mexican soldiers attacked Geronimo's village while he and the rest of the men were in town trading. Geronimo came home to find his mother, wife and all three of his children dead. Those Mexican soldiers had made a big mistake. They ticked off one bad hombre of an Apache. Geronimo took revenge.

His name was actually Goyale, but on one engagement, amid a hail of bullets he passed among a bunch of Mexican soldiers, carving them up with his knife. The Mexicans were so terrified, they prayed to Saint Jerome to save them. The Anglos hearing Jeromeo thought Geronimo was his name and it stuck.

For the next 28 years, he waged war on Mexicans and Americans. In the end, he led a band of 36 men, women, and children, evading Mexican and American troops for over a year. He was the most famous Native American of the time and deemed the "worst Indian who ever lived" by the white settlers.

In 1886 Geronimo surrendered to American soldiers. He was imprisoned for seven years, and eventually put on the reservation at Fort Sill, Oklahoma. Enjoying celebrity status, he appeared in the World's Fair in St. Louis and rode in President Theodore Roosevelt's inaugural parade in 1905. He was never allowed to return to the land of his birth.

Along the way he enjoyed seven wives and sired many children. What a man!

TEXAS JOINS THE UNION – MEXICAN WAR

Texas joined the Union December 29, 1845. In anticipation of Texas joining, in July of that year, US General Zachary Taylor requested any militia forces from Texas to join his army to invade Mexico. The first Texas soldiers were the Rangers under the command of Captain Samuel Walker. Texans alone could not put a significant army in the field, but as part of the United States Army, they had precisely what they wanted, a chance to fight Mexico on favorable terms and on Mexican soil.

General Taylor asked for two companies of Rangers to act as scouts. What he got were men who fought with a bloody ferocity in many battles. "Los Diablos Tejanos" the Mexicans called them, (The Texas Devils). These Devil Rangers were heavily armed and had no reservations about killing Mexicans. The Comanche had taught them well.

They were trouble for General Taylor. They had no discipline as he knew it. He could not manage them and sent some of them home. He noted that in every expedition the Rangers had killed Mexicans unnecessarily. Taylor wrote, "There is scarcely a crime that has not been reported to me as committed by them." But the army continued to use them because they were so successful.

Ranger operations became guerrilla combat. Keeping in front of the army, not only kept the road open for the regular forces, but they chased the Mexicans into their mountain hideouts, taking no prisoners. They wore outlandish costumes and sported long beards inciting terror in the Mexicans by their savage appearance. Each man carried a rifle and a pair of Colt revolvers.

Arriving in Mexico City, some civilians came out to see the devil rangers they had heard so much about. Two threw rocks at them. They were shot dead.

An observer described the Rangers: "They rode, some standing upright, some sideways, some, faced to the rear, some on horses, some on asses, some on mustangs, and some on mules."

The war with Mexico went on from 1846 to 1848 in the wake of the U.S. Annexation of Texas, which Mexico considered part of its territory despite the 1836 Texas Revolution.

American forces invaded New Mexico and California. Another American army captured Mexico City, forcing Mexico to agree to the sale of its northern territories to the U.S. The major consequence of the war was the forced Mexican Cession of the territories of California, Arizona, Nevada, and New Mexico to the U.S. in exchange for $18 million. Mexico accepted the Rio Grande as its national border.

Texas is big now, but imagine the size of her as a republic. Back then the Panhandle had a panhandle.
Author Mike Blakley

GALVESTON

The independent nation of Texas in 1836 was land-rich but money poor. During its ten year existence until it joined the United States it struggled. This was not true of thirty mile long Galveston Island. Even before the middle of the 1850's the city of Galveston was the queen city of Texas. In 1854 a few powerful men took control of the docks and were able to charge high fees for cargo passing in and out of Texas. In 1860, two thirds of the 300,000 bales of cotton leaving Texas went through Galveston and eleven million dollars of other goods. A million dollars was a lot back them. It cost five dollars to book passage to New Orleans. Ships were leaving daily for New York, Boston, New Orleans and Europe.

To get cotton to Galveston, some enterprising men would cut timber to make a raft, stack bales of cotton on it and float it down the Trinity or Brazos rivers. Arriving at the coast, the timber was worth almost as much as the cotton. In the mid 1850's Stern wheelers took over on the rivers and Galveston was processing forty-seven thousand board feet of lumber daily. Streets were paved with oyster shells and washed daily to keep the dust down. In one day in the spring of 1859, 450 tons of ice were offloaded on the docks of Galveston. The island produced most of its own food. 13,000 head of cattle lived there.

Banks were not allowed. Large stores printed their own money and twelve percent interest was charged to borrow money by those who would loan. This was twice what one would pay in New York.

Yellow fever took 400 to 500 lives a year. Small children were especially vulnerable. Half the babies born in Galveston would die of yellow fever. No one understood how it was spread. Of the thousand young people on the island, only two hundred went to school.

In the 1850's, leading up to the Civil War, there were 1,500 slaves on the island. Galveston Island was the best place to be a slave. The power elite considered it not proper to flaunt their wealth directly. Instead they dressed their slaves in rich silks and let them ride around town in fine carriages.

In 1817 when pirate Jean Lafitte was based on Galveston Island, selling slaves for a dollar a pound and pillaging shipping in the Gulf of Mexico, the entrance to the harbor was restricted. A sandbar prevented deep-drafter vessels from entering Galveston Bay. Their cargo had to be carried to port using barges or small boats. In 1874, work on two parallel jetties at the entrance to Galveston Bay began. The jetties consisted of huge granite boulders extending for thousands of feet into the Gulf. One jetty was connected to the eastern end of Galveston Island, while the other extended from the western tip of the Bolivar Peninsula. This concentrated the bay's outflow into a relatively narrow space carrying sediment farther out into the Gulf of Mexico. A deep channel into the bay was thus naturally created and maintained.

Houston, twenty five miles up Galveston Bay and the Houston Ship Chanel eventually took the shine off Galveston by charging more reasonable duty fees. A rail road through Houston connected it to all parts of the United States and Houston was more protected from storms. The 1900 hurricane dealt a blow to Galveston from which it never fully recovered.

CIVIL WAR

Passions ran high leading up to the Civil War. In 1861 Sam Houston, as Governor of Texas, campaigned hard to talk his fellow Texans out of joining the Confederacy, but the citizens didn't heed his warnings. They voted to secede and Houston was forced out of office. A bitter war followed ending in defeat of the South and then came reconstruction. It wasn't until March of 1870 that Texas reentered the union.

DEAD MAN'S HOLE

Sam Houston was not the only one in Texas against the war. Located off highway 401 near Marble Falls is a 155-foot-deep hole. Union sympathizers were thrown into this pit. That is like being tossed off a sixteen story building. Seventeen poor souls thus met their maker this way assuming Yankees indeed go to heaven.

CIVIL WAR BATTLES IN TEXAS

There were few battles fought in Texas in the Civil War. One of the more memorable was the Battle of Sabine Pass. Union forces were attempting to invade Texas by sea at Sabine Pass with 22 vessels and 5,000 soldiers. Lieutenant Richard W. Dowling with 42 men and six cannons were there to repel them. The battle lasted only 45 minutes during which the Texans took 350 Union soldiers prisoner, wounded or killed 68 more and crippled three of the Union gunboats. The Texans had been outnumbered 100 to 1, but suffered no losses. The Union Fleet retreated to New Orleans.

The last battle of the Civil War was fought at Palmetto Ranch near Brownsville on May 12, 1865. The South won only to learn Lee had surrendered on April 9th.

TERRY'S TEXAS RANGERS

In 1861, one of the early groups to sign up to fight from Texas was Terry's Texas Rangers. A sugar planter from Brazoria, Benjamin Terry, organized the regiment.

They were designated the 8th Texas Cavalry during the war, but called a variety of names, sometimes simply "The Texans."

The un-tested Terry's Rangers first fought near Woodsville, Kentucky, on December 17, 1861, when 181 Texans on horseback attacked and dispersed a much larger Union force. The battle lasted only four minutes in which Union casualties were 100 and the Rangers suffered a loss of twenty two. An astonished Union soldier later reported the Texans were quick as lightning, rode like Arabs, and fought like devils.

The regiment was not totally comprised of Texas Rangers, but there were enough seasoned Indian fighters who had fought in the Mexican war to determine the character of their fighting style. Naturally they came on horseback and each man carried two Colt pistols.

The Rangers distinguished themselves throughout the war by their skill and willingness to fight. They were called the "charging regiment," and were often called upon to act as shock troops. They fought at Shiloh, and were the main force for the charge at Fallen Timbers. These Texans led the way by sheer audacity, when General Forrest took Murfreesboro from a larger enemy force. They traveled hundreds of miles behind enemy lines to raid the enemy's sources of supply and communication. Alexander Shannon hand-picked men from the group to form the notorious Shannon's Scouts. This potent band harassed Sherman in his march across Georgia and into the Carolinas.

The final charge of Terry's Rangers was at Bentonville, North Carolina, on March 21, 1865, when General Hardee urgently called on Captain Matthews to check the Federal advance. After nearly four years of hard fighting, a hundred and fifty men, all that remained of the regiment charged into the Yankee infantry and forced their retreat.

The unit ended the war with 224 men from its original 1,600.

RECONSTRUCTION

Abe Lincoln was in favor of being lenient with the defeated south following the Civil War but he died. Johnson followed with the same attitude, but a bunch of hard noses in Congress were out to punish the South. When Johnson vetoed their legislation, they threatened to impeach him.

In the end, Congress prevailed. The southern states were put under military rule. Jeff Davis, president of the Confederacy, was imprisoned for two years, and Captain Henry Wirz, the commandant of the prison camp in Andersonville, Georgia was executed for war crimes as probably he should have been. 13,000 Union soldiers died in that prison.

Carpet Baggers (recent arrivals from the North) and Scallywags, (Southerners who supported Reconstruction) took advantage of the situation. Plantations were confiscated because the owners had paid taxes to the wrong country, the Confederacy, or for any other charge. Blacks who could not read and had no background for leadership suddenly found themselves armed and running the South. They could vote or run for office. The South was destitute. Cities and infrastructure were in shambles, livestock depleted, farm machinery gone, many great plantations taxed out of existence. They could not afford to hire the freed blacks. A system of share croppers evolved.

It took generations for the South to rebuild. This was not necessary. Whites in the south were bitter and formed organizations such as the Ku Klux Klan. They passed Jim Crow laws, and levied poll taxes, determined to maintain white supremacy. Many blacks were murdered or assaulted. With Lincoln's more lenient policies, it would have been different. Texas was not permitted to have representation in the US Congress until 1870.

The resentment lasted for generations. Growing up in Texas in the 1940's, I remember a civics teacher in middle school railing on about what rotten people Yankees were. "Don't ever go up north!" he admonished. Reconstruction was associated with Republicans. Texas voted for Democrats for generations.

Three new amendments to the constitution were passed. The Thirteenth Amendment abolished slavery. The Fourteenth Amendment was added to grant citizenship to the former slaves. It was worded so that anyone born in the United States except visitors and Indians on reservations had all the rights of citizenship. The amendment today causes problems because expectant mothers cross our southern border to have their babies and thus obtain the right of citizenship for their babies. The Fifteenth Amendment decreed the right to vote could not be denied because of race, color or previous condition of servitude.

EMANCIPATION PROCLAIMATION

Lincoln freed the slaves in his emancipation proclamation January first, 1863, but it didn't help the slaves in confederate Texas. The Civil War was over April 9, 1865, but no slave went free in Texas. It wasn't until June nineteenth that Federal General Gordon Granger came to Galveston and declared the slaves free. To this day blacks celebrate "June Teenth" in Texas. The whites called it "Nigger Day" as they watched the annual black parades. Of course, blacks still had to ride on the back of the bus, and go to the back door of restaurants if they wanted to eat and use the "Colored" restrooms and drinking fountains if there were any provided. I remember it well. It didn't get any better until the Civil Rights movement in the 1960's.

CATTLE DRIVES

Adding to the Texas mystique is the memory of the cattle drives. They were the stuff of myth, legend and movies. After the Civil War, men returning from battle found a destitute Texas. No federal government was there to offer meal vouchers or unemployment compensation. There were few opportunities for raising money. However, over five million Texas longhorn cattle wandered loose. By 1867, the long horn cattle had evolved in Texas from various European breeds getting loose and inbreeding over three hundred years since the Spanish first tried to settle Texas. They were lean, wily, rangy beasts that could survive on sparse grass. If not walked too fast on the trail, some even gained weight. The long horns had developed immunity to Texas fever spread by a tick.

A mature cow would fetch $4 in Texas but $40 up North. A few cows were driven all the way to Chicago, some to California, some even to New York City. Problems arose from that disease carrying tick. When long horns were driven through new territory, the local cows died of the fever. Farmers soon blocked their passage. This gave birth to the Chisolm Trail which was roughly today's I-35. From various origins in South Texas, the herds merged on the trail and progressed up past San Antonio, Waco, and

Fort Worth, or Dallas. It continued on to Red River Station in Montague county. Then they followed the wagon tracks of an Indian trader named Jesse Chisolm. Arrangements were agreed upon to allow the herders up a narrow corridor to the rail head at Abilene, Kansas where the cows were loaded aboard trains.

Over six million cows were herded up the Chisolm Trail in a seventeen year period from 1867 to 1884. The memory lives on as something uniquely Texas. It wasn't that long ago. I once met a man who recalls witnessing the last cattle drive through down-town Dallas. Crossing rivers, dealing with rustlers, snakes, and Indians hardens a man. Texans, like the long horns evolved by natural selection. The strong and self-reliant prospered. The weak retreated back east.

Origin of Maverick

In the mid 1850's, a rancher named Maverick built up a sizable herd of long horns. During the civil War days, he allowed his calf crop to go unbranded. As a result, by the end of the war, there were thousands of his cattle without brands roaming the Texas countryside. In Maverick's area, folks would say, "there is a Maverick:," when referring to an unbranded cow. The term was taken up by others, and in a short time it was in general use throughout the cattle range country in Texas for an unbranded cow.

Rustling

Rustling became a well-organized business in many sections of the range country. The problem became so bad that the ranchers were forced to deal with the situation. Committees were organized to handle the rustlers. Those committees would notify a rustler to leave. If the man ignored the demand, the committee would catch the accused and hold a trial.

One member of the committee would act as the judge, another, the prosecutor. The evidence for and against would be heard. The verdict would be rendered. Many were sentenced to be hanged and the hanging would take place on the spot. Some of the accused were turned loose with a warning and given another chance.

We still execute a lot of criminals here in Texas, but it isn't the same. Lawyers appeal and it takes years and a fortune to get anyone to the death chamber. It is cheaper to let the guilty rot in jail for life.

My friend, Casey, tells me we bury dead lawyers seven feet deep in Texas instead of the usual six feet because down deep lawyers are good people.

If the King's English was good enough for Jesus, it is good enough for me.
Ma Ferguson, Texas Governor

TEXAS COWBOY BOOTS

When I moved to the country, folks told me I needed to raise cows. I bought five pregnant cows. Then I went back up to Dallas for a family gathering. The guys were wearing cowboy boots. Here I was a big Texas cattle baron and I didn't even own a pair. So I bought a pair of genuine Justin Boots. I like wearing boots and rarely wear anything else now. It is so-o-o Texan. The Texas-style boot was specially designed for cattle men.

When mounting and, especially, dismounting, the treadless leather sole of the boot facilitates easy insertion and removal of the foot into the stirrup. The toe is a bit narrowed to make it easier to insert.

While in the saddle, the tall heel minimizes the risk of the foot sliding forward through the stirrup, which could be dangerous. If a rider falls from a horse but his boot gets caught in the stirrup, there is risk the horse could panic and run off, dragging the cowboy, causing injury or death.

The tall leather shaft of the boot holds the boot in place and helps prevent a rider from being dragged. His body weight could pull his foot out of the boot if he falls off. The shaft also protects the lower leg and ankle from chafing on the stirrup. While afoot, the shaft protects the leg from thorns, and snakes.

In the covered wagon days, if a baby was born in Texarkana while the family was crossing into the Lone Star State, by the time they reached El Paso, the baby would be in the third grade.

Texas Author Wallace O Charlton

JOHN HARDIN, BILL LONGLEY, DOC HOLLIDAY, BELLE STAR

JOHN WESLEY HARDIN

Everyone is bigger and badder in Texas. Example—John Wesley Hardin. 1853 – 1895. He was the greatest gunman in western history. By his own count, he killed forty men though this gambler, cowboy, quick draw artist always felt justified. He considered his gun fights fair against other armed men. He never joined a gang or killed for hire. Hardin was a well-educated gentleman and loving father who tried to instill high ideals in his children. It is just that people kept threatening him and got shot for the trouble. Some folks just need killing I guess.

During the Civil War, Wes Hardin and his brother were too young to go to war. They stayed home to mind the farm. By age nine, he was known for his fast draw and deadly accuracy. At age twelve he knifed a classmate who insulted a fat girl in his class.

Hardin's mother told him not to carry a gun, but he didn't listen. Wes was fifteen when he and his cousin challenged a freed slave to a wrestling match. They put the black man down and scratched his face in the process. The next day the furious black ambushed the two cousins with a club and Hardin shot him dead. It was during reconstruction and three Yankee soldiers were sent out to bring him in. Hardin killed all three in a shootout. Shooting lawmen was a no, no even then. Now Wes was a fugitive.

The following year he and a cousin killed two more union soldiers who came to get them. By now Wes, aged sixteen, was expert at poker and always won in quick draw competition. On Christmas Day, 1869, he won $100 in a poker game against Arkansas gambler, Jim Bradley. Bradley pulled a knife and chased him outside. Hardin returned with a borrowed piston and shot Bradley between the eyes.

Hardin's preacher father sent his wanted son to live with an uncle. Wes killed two more men on the way, and then while attending a circus he caused a circus roustabout to cut his lip. The irate man drew on Hardin and Wes had to shoot him.

A pretty young girl took a shine to Hardin, but when he came calling, the girl's rejected boyfriend demanded Hardin's money or his life. It was a bad idea for the boyfriend who died from a gunshot wound to the head.

This is the way Wes Hardin's life went. Folks kept getting shot around him, especially those sent out to bring him in.

On a trail drive to Abilene, Kansas he killed ten people, making a total of 23 victims before he was 23 years old.

Wesley Hardin's life of drinking, gambling, killing and running from the law went on for 42 years. Then Constable John Selman came through the Saloon door in El Paso and shot him before he could draw his gun. It wasn't a fair fight. If I were going up against Hardin, I don't believe I would go for fairness either.

BILL LONGLEY

Two years older than John Hardin, Bill Longley was perhaps just as fast with a gun, but even more savage. He killed because he enjoyed it and he particularly liked shooting blacks. His first shootout was during reconstruction, when he was fifteen, a black policeman insulter his father and Langley shot him. His life was similar to John Hardin's. It was one of odd jobs, killing, in and out of jail, and living on the run. He was Texas' most wanted outlaw when captured the last time and sentenced to hang. Longley protested that it wasn't fair. He had only killed twenty two men and John Hardin had killed a lot more and only got a life sentence once when Hardin went to trial. Reading about his exploits makes me suspect Bill Longley just enjoyed the adrenalin rush of killing folks.

DOC HOLLIDAY

"Doc" Holliday was born in Griffin, Georgia in 1852. At age 19 he went to school in Philadelphia, receiving his degree in Dental Surgery in March of 1872.

Shortly after beginning his dental practice, Holliday was diagnosed with tuberculosis and given only a few months to live. Thinking a move to the South West might be a healthier place; he moved to Dallas in September of 1873 and opened a dental practice.

He started gambling and found it more profitable since patients were few because of his ongoing cough. In May of 1874, Holliday was indicted for illegal gambling. He was arrested again in Dallas in January 1875 after a shoot-out with a saloon-keeper. He moved his offices to Denison, Texas and after being fined for, "gaming" in Dallas, he left the state.

Holliday had many more such disagreements, fueled by a hot temper and believing death by gun or knife was better than by tuberculosis.

In 1877, Holliday was in fort Griffin, Texas, where he met Wyatt Earp. A friendship cemented in 1878 in Dodge City, Kansas, when Holliday defended Earp against a handful of cowboys out to kill Earp. Holliday was a deadly shooter and owned the bar. He approached from another angle to cover the group with a gun, and threatened to shoot. Earp credited Holliday with saving his life that day.

On July 19, 1879, Holliday and John Joshua Webb were seated in a saloon in Las Vegas, New Mexico when mike Gordon tried to persuade one of the saloon girls to leave her job and come away with him. When she refused, Gordon stormed outside and shot into the building. Holliday went out and killed him.

Holliday is best remembered for participating with Wyatt Earp at the famed "GUNFIGHT AT THE O K CORRAL." He later split with Earp and moved to Glenwood Springs, Colorado. His health deteriorated, and he died of tuberculosis on November 8, 1887.

OUTLAW BELLE STAR

Born Myra Belle Shirley, Belle Star drifted in and out of Texas as a young woman. She graduated from the Carthage, Missouri Female Academy where she leaned the three R's, Greek, Latin, Hebrew and how to play the Piano, but she had a reputation as a scrapper. She preferred horses and the outdoors. Her older brother, Bud, taught her how to shoot and to despise Yankees. Belle came to Texas when she was fifteen with her parents and settled near Dallas. She married Jim Reed. They had two children. Jim was often in trouble with the law. He was thrown in jail in a small Texas town. Belle came to visit him wearing a long black dress. Jim left his cell wearing the dress. The jailer later was surprised to find Belle in the cell instead. She demanded to be released as she had done nothing wrong. They kept her a few days and released her. Jim was always on the lam. The couple dealt in stolen horses and other shady deals. Sheriff

Nichols of Dallas County put Jim in jail and Belle told the sheriff to release him or she would kill him. The next day Nichols was shot dead and not long after, Jim was released. Stories of Belle's adventures abound. She is credited with torturing a rich Indian until he gave her $30,000.

She had an encounter with a banker who thought a late night meeting at his bank would be a love encounter but instead ended with him being bound and gagged and the bank being robbed.

Dressed as a man, she joined Reed and others in a stage coach robbery and was left behind. When the U.S. Marshall questioned her, she gave her name as Rosa McComus, a woman she didn't like.

John Morris feigned friendship with Jim Reed, traveled with him, and then killed him for the reward on Jim's head. The only one around who could identify the body was Belle. She examined the corpse and announced it was not that of her husband. This left John Morris trying to beat a murder rap of an unknown man.

Belle Star was rumored to have many lovers, some outlaws, some law men, and an Indian named Blue duck, but she usually preferred the outlaws. She was flamboyant, and larger than life as befitting a Texas lady outlaw.

REUNION TOWER

LA REUNION

I grew up in Dallas, but I never heard of the La Reunion society. They were a bunch of Europeans back in 1855 that came to Texas to form a sort of utopian socialist community. They landed on the coast, put their stuff on ox carts and walked the some 250 miles to an area just outside of Dallas.

The location was not good land for crops. They had few skills for farming and the weather threw them a nasty curve. There came a freak blizzard in May of 1856 followed by a drought then a plague of grass hoppers. They spoke a different language than the local settlers, had a different religion and form of government. They were soon starving. Some returned to Europe. Those who stayed eventually moved in to Dallas doubling the population of the fledging town.

Though these colonists were poor farmers, some brought other needed skills. One man opened the first butcher shop in Dallas. Another built the first brewery. Maxime Guillot established a carriage factory making

Dallas a center for carriage and harness-making that lasted until the automobile came along a half century later.

In recent years Reunion Tower and Reunion Arena grace the Dallas skyline, named after the Reunion society. In time these settlers morphed into Texans like so many others.

LAW WEST OF THE PECOS

Roy Bean was born in Kentucky. As a young man he floated down the Mississippi to New Orleans. There he got in trouble, so he fled to Texas where a brother lived. He and his brother started a business in Mexico but Roy was run out of town after killing a man. He went to San Diego where another brother lived and was soon thrown in jail. He broke out of jail and headed up to Los Angeles where another brother ran a saloon. You may begin to see a pattern here. In Los Angeles, he was hanged for killing a man, but a lady friend cut the rope before he died. Finding California an unfriendly place, Roy made his way back to Texas.

He spent the next twenty years in San Antonio where he got married and had four children before his wife left him, claiming abuse. He spent most of his time as a bar tender and a teamster hauling goods to as far away as El Paso. For a while he was in the milk business, but watered down the milk to make more profit. When a minnow was found in some milk he sold, he explained to the judge that the cow must have swallowed that minnow when it drank from the river.

In 1870, The Southern Pacific Railroad was laying track all the way from San Antonio to California. A friend suggested he go out to the construction site and open a saloon. The wife of a store owner in his neighborhood offered $900 to buy up all his belongings if he would just leave and never come back. Now at age 56, he started on a new career.

With his $900, Roy bought a tent, ten barrels of whiskey, some crackers and canned goods and headed out. There were eight thousand men within twenty miles where the track was being laid. A Ranger described the men building the line as the worst lot of roughs, gamblers, robbers, and pickpockets he had ever seen and asked for local law jurisdiction to clean up the construction camps. The Commissioners' Court of Pecos County appointed Roy Bean as Justice of the Peace. Now, that makes sense, doesn't it?

After a couple of moves, Roy set up his saloon/court room squatting on the railroad right away at Langtry which he had no legal right to, but he stayed there for the next 20 years.

The Judge had a few simple rules. No appeals, no hung juries, and he would pocket all fines. One of Bean's first big decisions involved an Irishman who playfully told a Chinaman to duck, but the man failed to do so and was shot dead. The Irish drank a lot of the Judge's whiskey. The Chinese did not. Bean's verdict was that his only law book defined homicide as killing a human being, but it didn't say anything about the killing of a Chinaman. NOT GUILTY. A ROUND OF DRINKS FOR THE HOUSE PAID FOR BY THE DEFENDANT.

Trains stopped for twenty minutes at Langtry to fill up with water, just time enough for thirsty passengers to get off and visit the Judge's saloon.

After moving out of the tent and building his permanent saloon, he sentenced a man arrested for disturbing the peace to painting signs. JUDGE ROY BEAN, COURT HOUSE, SALOON, THE LAW WEST OF THE PECOS, WHISKEY, WINE AND BEER, THE JERSEY LILLY.

Judge Bean was first elected as justice of the peace in 1884. He was reelected every two years after that until 1896 when he lost to Jesus

Torres, but he refused to give up his seal and law book and continued to try cases.

There was no jail in Langtry. All cases were finable and defendants were chained to a tree until trial. Each Monday the Judge would clear the docket. Jurors appointed by the Judge were always good bar customers and were expected to have a drink or two during recess. Fines were usually the exact amount in the defendant's pockets.

During his reign, he sentenced two men to be hanged. One was a Mexican rustler deserving to be hanged. The other offender was a young man who stole a wallet and pistol. He stood defiantly before the Judge shouting obscenities and threatening the Judge's son with a knife. He was sentenced to hang. A noose was placed over his head and the rope thrown over a box car. Then someone took the noose off his head and told him to run like hell.

A Bean wedding was five dollars. Roy would end the ceremony with "And may God have mercy on your souls." Divorces cost ten dollars though he was not officially authorized to perform them.

When a dead man was brought in with a pistol and $40 in his pocket, the Judge fined the corpse the $40 for carrying a concealed weapon.

Patrons stopping by for a drink needed the correct amount to pay for it. Roy never gave change. If a customer made too much fuss about wanting his change, the Judge would fine him for disturbing the peace.

Liquor salesmen who stopped by to sell supplies were expected to buy a round for the house then pay for it by counting the empty bottles. Bean kept a few extra empty bottles around to add to the count.

As Judge Bean's reputation grew, people would flock to his saloon to watch his outrageous behavior. He became a Texas institution.

In spite of the fact that Judge Roy Bean was a murderer and a thief, he was not all bad. Most of his profits in later years went to feeding the hungry drifters or for medicines for those who could not afford them. He supplied fire wood for widows and for the local school house. Finding fire wood was no small feat among the scrub brush that grew in the area.

Who knows what Texas might have been like without dedicated men like the Judge to bring justice to the Wild West?

OLD RIP

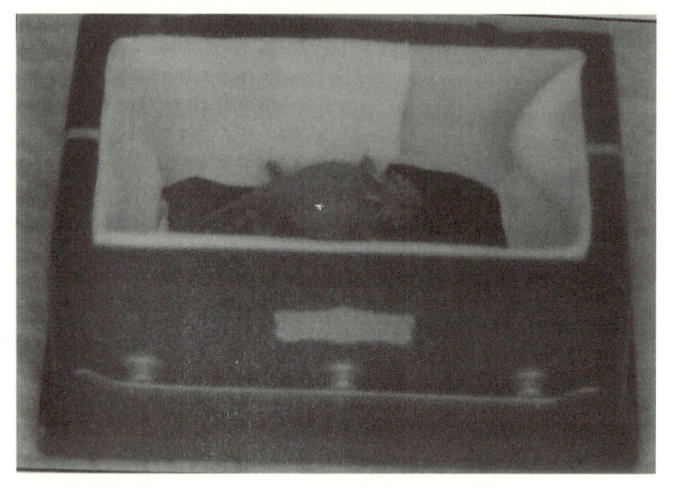

Every Texan worth his salt knows the story of "Old Rip," the horned toad entombed in the cornerstone of the Eastland County Courthouse in 1875.

When a new court house was planned in 1897, the old structure was torn down. The corner stone opened up and Rip (short for Rip Van Winkle) was still alive.

In 1875, the Dallas Morning News had run an article speculating that perhaps horned toads could live for as long as a hundred years. So on a whim, Earnest E. Wood managed to get a horned toad (actually a Texas lizard) placed in the corner stone of the court house.

When the old court house was being torn down in 1897 to make way for a new court house, Wood reminded everyone about the horned toad.

Boyce House, editor of the Eastland Argus Tribune played it up in his paper to the point that people came from miles around to witness the opening of the corner stone.

In order to make sure there was no fraud regarding Old Rip, several of the town's most trusted citizens were on hand to certify if in fact Rip was actually there and alive. He was.

Now there were court proceedings to determine who owned Rip. The lizard was taken on tour to St. Louis, New York City, Washington D.C. and points in-between. He even met the President.

Rip lived another thirty two years. When he died, a local casket maker built a special casket with a glass top to display him and many people come to this day to view his remains in the Eastland County Courthouse.

FRENCH WINE HAS A TEXAS FLAVOR

The French have a reputation of being intolerably snobbish, especially when it comes to their wine. In the United States, the French varieties of grapes could only be grown in California due to a nematode (round worm) prevalent in the States that the European vines had no resistance to. American varieties had developed immunity.

Someone took American grape vines to Europe to see how they would grow there. The nematode was in the roots and quickly spread, killing off the French wine industry in the late 1800's. Fortunately Thomas V. Munson of Denison, Texas had been experimenting with crossing the European and American varieties to develop nematode resistant varieties. He was able to supply the hybrids to reestablish the European vineyards.

So when you drink a glass of fine imported French wine, know you are enjoying Texas grapes. Texans have merely hired the French to raise and process them into wine for us. Better yet, buy from a Texas winery.

DR PEPPER

We would, of course, expect in such things as soft drink manufacturers for Texas to lead the way. In 1885 pharmacist Charles Alderton in Waco, Texas, concocted the drink he originally called "The Waco."

It was later changed to Dr Pepper. Wade Morrison was the owner of Alderton's pharmacy and he suggested the name change to impress Dr. Charles Pepper, the father of the girl Morrison hoped to marry. It didn't work. He still didn't get the girl.

Originally the drink was promoted as a medicinal drink for better health and regularity. Thus they coined the slogan, "Drink Dr Pepper at ten, two, and four."

Dr. Pepper came out in 1885, Coke in 1886, and Pepsi in 1898. Rumor has it that Dr Pepper is made from Prune Juice. Actually it is apricot juice. Dr Pepper is the only non-cola drink of the three.

The Dr Pepper museum is located at 300 S. Fifth in Waco.

TEXAS RAILROADS

A map of Anderson County at the turn of the century shows rivers and railroads but no highways. There were none. Freight moved on the rivers until the railroads took over. River boats made it up the Trinity River as far as present day Palestine, Texas. The last riverboat up the Trinity carried railroad track.

When I drive to Tyler via the back roads I pass a sign announcing Fincastle, but there is no town. It died when the railroad by-passed it.

Further East is the town of Jefferson, a former hub for moving cotton by riverboat to New Orleans. For a fee, Jay Gould offered to run his railroad through Jefferson, but the city fathers saw no reason to go to the expense. Today Jefferson is only a tourist town celebrating days gone by. Progress passed it by without the railroad.

In 1896, a ticket agent named Crush working for the Katy Railroad noticed how fascinated people were with train wrecks. Why not stage a train wreck with two steam engines pulling freight cars plowing head on into each other? People would come from miles around. And people did. The railroad built a spur north of Waco and a train station proudly boasting the name of CRUSH, TEXAS. For $2 round trip people could come from anywhere in Texas to witness the spectacle. Lemonade stands and souvenir venders set up shop. Over forty thousand people were in the stands. Two vintage steam engines ready to be scrapped anyway squared off and plowed into each other each going 60 miles an hour. Mr. Crush's idea was brilliant. The rail road and the vendors made money and the witnesses received more than they bargained for. What could possibly be the down side? It was spectacular. Unfortunately, the boilers in those steam engines blew up on impact sending jagged metal in all directions. Three people were killed and many more injured. OOPS! The tracks were taken up and the depot torn down. Mr. Crush was fired and Crush, Texas is now just a cow pasture.

ROSS PEROT

Texas continually gives birth to giants. Among these was Ross Perot who graduated from the Naval Academy, was a salesman for IBM, and then founded Electronic Data Systems (EDS) making him one of the richest men in America.

In 1992 he ran for president as an Independent. He didn't win. What a pity. Maybe he could have drained the swamp that is Washington, D.C. In 1978 two of Perot's EDS executives were taken hostage by the Iranian government. When attempts to resolve the situation through diplomatic channels failed, Perot acted independently. Remembering retired Col. Bull Simons, Perot called him and asked him if he would organize and lead the rescue of his men. Simons organized a team and told Perot, "See if the U.S. Embassy will allow these men to receive refuge at the embassy when we get them out of prison." When Perot talked to the American ambassador he said, "No," and two hours later, the Iranian security forces were tearing up the town looking for Perot. That is your government working for you. Simons then said, "Perot, I want you to go to the prison where the men are held. Visit with them, and tell them what our plan of action is, so that they know where the rendezvous point is and what they are supposed to do.

Perot replied, "Colonel, the Iranians are still looking for me."

"One branch of the Iranian government is looking for you, but another branch of the government runs the prison. They don't talk to one another. They won't know anything about you at the prison," Simons argued.

If Bull Simons tells you to do it, you do it. A rescue team member drove Perot to the prison where the two EDS executives were being held. The courage it must have taken for Perot to go to that prison when he was being hunted by the Iranian government says much about the man. It is the stuff Texas giants are made of: courage, resourcefulness, loyalty, and follow-through. He was determined to go the distance for his people. There were at least a hundred camera crews at the prison. Perot walked past them and they ignored him. He went in, walked up to the reception room and there was former Attorney General Ramsey Clark, sitting there talking to the general in charge of the prison. Ramsey leaned forward and pointed at Perot, and spoke to the general. The general politely arranged for him to meet with Paul Chiapparone and Bill Gaylord, the two detained EDS executives.

The man who actually led the rescue at the prison was an Iranian systems engineer working for EDS. They called him "Rashid." Simons roamed the streets of Tehran and saw large numbers of Iranian terrorist teams. Simons told Rashid to create an Iranian "terrorist" team so that Rashid, as their leader, could attend the morning meetings. There were many such teams all over Tehran who would meet each morning to plan their daily activities. Team leaders also attended, so Rashid was able to go to the meetings. Rashid formed a team to infiltrate the revolutionary movement.

Before the jailbreak actually occurred, Simons told Rashid, "See if you can bribe the police chief to leave open the police armory, where all the weapons are stored." Rashid paid them $100, less than the cost of a pistol, to leave the police armory open. Rashid and his team attended the next morning meeting with a large cache of weapons. Rashid distributed weapons around the room, and shouted, "Gasre Prison is our Bastille. It is our responsibility to free the thousands of political prisoners."

An hour later, 30,000 terrorists stormed the prison. The guards never fired a shot. 12,000 prisoners escaped so the two EDS men could also get free.

The team, with the two EDS executives drove over 500 miles to Turkey. They were within 30 miles of the border when a group of Islamic revolutionaries stopped the vehicles, pulled Simons out, and started hitting him. Simons pulled a note out of his pocket and handed it to them. The note read, "These people are friends of the revolution; please show them courtesy and escort them safely to the border," signed, Commandant of the Tehran Islamic Revolutionary Committee. The note sported an impressive seal. If you were to read it closely, it said, "Rezaieh Religious School: Founded 1344." It wasn't an official Revolutionary seal, but it got the men home to their wives and families.

PEROT QUOTES

In plain Texas talk, do the right thing.

If you see a snake, just kill it—don't appoint a committee on snakes.

Failures are like skinned knees, painful but superficial.

If you can't stand a little sacrifice and you can't stand a trip across the desert with limited water, we're never going to straighten this country out.

War has rules, mud wrestling has rules—politics has no rules.

Punishing honest mistakes stifles creativity, I want people moving and shaking the earth and they're going to make mistakes.

TEXAS OIL

After 1868, John D. Rockefeller controlled Standard Oil and had a virtual monopoly on petroleum that replaced whale oil with kerosene for lighting houses. Gasoline was thrown away as a dangerous by-product.

The monopoly was broken in 1894 when the city fathers in Corsicana, Texas, drilled for water to supply the town. They drilled two wells and got oil each time, so they built a refinery and developed the first commercial oil field in Texas. It was the birth of Texaco and the oil boom in Texas.

Soon after, Spindletop came in near Beaumont on the Texas coast. Prospectors were trying to get enough oil to fire bricks at a local brick factory. They got more oil than anyone knew what to do with. By 1902, the annual production was 17.5 million barrels. The price of oil dropped to three cents a barrel while a glass of water locally was five cents. It gave birth to Gulf Oil, Sun Oil, Mobile, and ESSO. Texas oil transformed transportation around the world. Enter the automobile, the airplane, and diesel locomotives. Our Texas coal mines at Thurber shut down as railroads converted to diesel . Texas was no more an agrarian society, Texas Was Oil!

The boom attracted scam artists peddling worthless leases. Prostitutes, gamblers and liquor dealers, all vied for workers' paychecks. Portable jails on wheels were brought in while permanent facilities could be built in the latest boom town.

In 1839, the Congress of the independent nation of Texas set aside 50 leagues (221.400 acres) of land for the endowment of a university. In 1858, the area was increased to a million acres, with the stipulation that it be good agricultural land. Writers of the Constitution of 1876 saw no need to appropriate arable land for an as-yet-nonexistent university. The first million acres in the endowment were relocated in the wilderness of far-west Texas. When the University of Texas opened in 1883, the legislature added a second million acres in the west. The fledgling university was then backed by an endowment of a vast amount of land of dubious value. It turned out that the Permian Basin is in this land with its vast oil deposit.

The Santa Rita No. 1, discovery well of the Big Lake field, gushed in on May 28, 1923, in Reagan County. It was drilled on University Lands. Within a year, there were 17 producing wells in the Big Lake Field, and the University of Texas became a very wealthy school as this second major Texas oil field came in. Texas University was suddenly a very rich university. Tuition was next to nothing.

The discovery of oil in East Texas was a long-held dream. By 1925, there had been 17 failed attempts. Then came seventy year old (Dad) Joiner, a native of Alabama. He had moved to Oklahoma in 1897, where he made and lost two fortunes in oil before moving to Texas. In 1926 he bought up several thousand East Texas oil leases. Joiner's drilling rig was rusty pipes, with a sawmill boiler fueled by old tires and cordwood.

His first well, the Daisy Miller Bradford No. 1, was abandoned when a drill bit jammed. The derrick was moved 100 feet. This second well site was abandoned because of equipment failure too. On the third try, the derrick was moved 300 feet before a beam broke, so the well was drilled at that location beginning in May 1929. Had the derrick been moved to the selected spot, Joiner would have drilled a dry hole. On October. 3, 1930, drillers brought in the first East Texas oil well, the Daisy Bradford

Number 3, soon followed by two others within the field. They had hit the largest area of oil deposits known anywhere at that time.

Within months, Joiner was embroiled in numerous lawsuits. Another Texas oil man, H.L. Hunt, bought out Joiner's interest in the wells. Although the giant East Texas Oilfield made many millionaires, "Dad" Joiner died not a rich man.

Oil operators fought regulation, and sold stolen oil illegally. Unscrupulous producers would tap into someone else's flow line, or put a by-pass on his own. When crime and violence overwhelmed the local police, Kilgore's mayor called the Texas Rangers. In true Texas fashion, Ranger "Lone Wolf" Gonzaullas answered the call. He shucked his ranger garb and went about town as any other looking to make a quick buck. In this way, he learned who the local criminals were.

Two weeks later, he led a raid with other rangers and Kilgore police netting 300 misfits. Kilgore's jail was unfinished. The law breakers were hooked to a long heavy chain. Then for almost a month, Gonzaullas averaged 100 arrests a day.

Texas still has the largest proven oil reserves in the United States. If Texas was an independent nation again, it would rank among the top ten producers in terms of proven oil and gas reserves.

Texas oil fueled both WWI and WWII and everything in-between. In the California Gold Rush, only a few prospered. In Texas many did. Fortunes were made and lost. It all added to the swagger of the Texas personality. With millionaires popping up all around, Texans tend to have the idea that anything is possible.

Over half the population of Texas was associated with the oil industry at one time or another and everyone benefited from it. Some wildcatters hit it extremely rich.

In Dallas, the need for a special department store arose to cater to the needs of the vast wealth pouring into Texas. This gave birth to Nieman Marcus where for Christmas you can order "his and her yachts."

Rich Texas oil men were too numerous to mention. Two, for example, were Bunker Hunt and Howard Hughes.

Nelson Bunker Hunt is best known as a oil billionaire whose fortune collapsed after he and his brother nearly cornered the world market in silver. Bunker Hunt played a significant role in the discovery and development of the oil fields in Libya.

Howard Hughes got in on the Texas oil boom when his father developed a better drill bit for oil wells. Howard inherited the Hughes Tool company when his father died. With millions of dollars in his pocket, he went to Hollywood and produced motion pictures, pioneered in aviation and slept with most of the motion picture's top stable of stars. He even owned 78% of Trans World Airlines.

Make no mistake, Texas oil lifted the whole world out of the horse and buggy and into cars and airplanes.

There are 254 counties in Texas and we pump oil out of 195 of them.

For a few precious moments...I am back in Old Texas, under a high sky—where all things are again possible and the wind blows free.
Larry L. King

OF COURSE, TEXANS BOAST OF BRINGING DOWN THE FIRST UFO

On April 19, 1897, the Dallas Morning News reported the crash of an air ship in Aurora, Texas, 30 miles northwest of Ft. Worth. This was six years before the Wright brothers made their historic first powered flight at Kitty Hawk. The article had a number of errors and many wrote it off as a hoax, but a cigar shaped air ship had been reported in various places in recent days including Illinois, Wisconsin, Indiana, and various towns in Texas. Newspapers reported sighting it in Denver and in East Texas on the same day.

The news article reported the craft had flown low over the town, crashed into Judge Proctor's windmill and exploded. The pilot was buried in the local cemetery.

Seventy six years later UFO enthusiasts sent a team to investigate. Jagged scraps of an unidentifiable metal were found at the scene indicating they had been ripped apart by a violent explosion. The grave marker had been stolen years before so the "alien" pilot's grave could not be located and exhumed. No eye witnesses could be found, but children of witnesses recounted the stories their parents had told them.

TEXAS LUMBER INDUSTRY

COMPANY STORE

Texas is not just a bunch of cowboys and oil men. There is a large Texas lumber industry. In 1982 lumber and forest products ranked among the top ten industries of the state. This is far below its dominant position at the beginning of the twentieth century. Then it was the state's largest manufacturing enterprise, first among Texas industries in generating income, and the largest employer. In 1907, the cut of more than 2.25 billion board feet of lumber was third largest in the United States.

Early workers spent long hours for low pay, and suffered frequent accidents. Logging and sawmilling are among the most hazardous of occupations. Workers toiled eleven hour days until about 1900, ten until World War I, and nine until World War II. Employers paid wages averaging $1.50 to $2.50 per day from around 1900 until the early 1920's.

To provide for the employees, often numbering several hundred, owners built company towns. In the isolated areas of East Texas, the mill owner was like a feudal baron dominating the lives of his workers and their families. In many operations the company paid the workers not in cash but in merchandise checks, scrip, or tokens that were worth face value only at the commissary to company store. Often the camps were tent cities where the logger and his wife and children all lived in a tent. Thus the dependence of the worker upon the company was nearly absolute. These conditions began to change after World War I.

1900 GALVESTON HURRICANE

Hurricanes regularly visit Texas. Indianola was hit in 1875 killing from 150 to 300 people and leaving eight buildings. Then in 1886 the town was struck again destroying everything. The survivors didn't bother to rebuild. They simply moved on. The worst natural disaster in American history was the 1900 hurricane that hit Galveston where 6,000 to 9,000 people died. Islanders were left so isolated from the mainland people were unable to report their plight to the outside world. The storm surge covered the entire island. Survivors were pressed into service disposing of the dead. Piles of the dead were loaded on barges, towed out to sea, and dumped. The bodies came floating back and deposited on the beaches on the next tide. Anyone robbing the corpses was shot and their remains disposed of with the rest. After the storm, Galvestonians brought in dredges and raised the island 17 feet. Surviving houses were raised on pilings and sand pumped in beneath. A concrete seawall was added for added protection.

The best book on the 1900 Galveston hurricane is "DEATH FROM THE SEA" by Herbert Mason Jr.

Mason relates story after story of survival, tragedy, and heroism. Consider the story of John Newman. This Newman must have been the grandfather of Alfred E. Newman. "What, me worry?" he didn't seek shelter, but waded the streets of Galveston in the wind and rain as the water continued to rise from the storm surge. As darkness fell, he wandered into a bar where he was standing in water up to his neck. The bar tender stood on the counter serving drinks and joking about the weather. Newman downed several whiskeys, bought a pint of brandy and went back outside.

The swirling water swept him down the street. When a large timber floated by, he latched onto it with one arm leaving the other free to take long pulls on the brandy. Meanwhile those around him perished. He could hear calls for help in the darkness.

At length he saw a light in the distance and made for it. He came to the upstairs of a boarding house and rapped on the door. The land lady opened the door and asked what he wanted.

Try to picture the scene, the worst storm ever, wind blowing at better than 130 miles an hour, rain peppering both of them like bullets. Newman still clutching his plank and his near empty bottle. "Good God, lady! What do you think I want?"

For thirty cents she gave him a room. He collapsed onto the bed in his wet clothes and went fast asleep in his drunken stupor.

When he awoke, next morning, the sun was shining. The rest of the house had blown away. He was the only survivor in the building. God protects drunks and little children. If you can find the book, read it. It is crammed full of such riveting true stories.

This experience, too, molded the Texas mindset. "When you reach the end of your rope, tie a knot and hang on. This too shall pass. There will be another oil well soon."

FIRST POWERED FLIGHT

Jan and I drove to Pittsburg, Texas a while back to see a replica of the first powered flying machine to carry a man aloft. It would be unthinkable that any but a Texan would claim the honor. The flight took place in 1902, a year before the Wright brothers made their first flight. The Reverend Burrell Cannon was inspired by a description of a flying machine described in the Bible in Ezekiel. Cannon's craft managed to fly 160 feet at an altitude of about twelve feet before the vibration threatened to tear the plane apart.

Reverend Cannon then loaded it on a rail car to take it to the St. Louis World's Fair. A storm in Texarkana ripped it apart leaving the Wright brothers to reap all the glory.

One night, when I was flying for American Airlines, the flight attendant came to the cockpit and said there was a passenger who wanted to talk to me. I went back and met a shriveled little old man standing in the aisle. "What can I do for you?" I asked. He said he wanted to show me his pilot's license. The thing was signed by Orval Wright. This guy was the second licensed pilot in the world! It hasn't been that long. The time-span between the Wright brothers and landing on the moon is amazingly short.

I love Texas because Texas is future-oriented, because Texans think anything is possible. Texans think big.
Senator Phil Gramm

MILITARY AVIATION BORN IN TEXAS

As one would naturally expect, military aviation was born in Texas on March 2, 1910 when Lieutenant Benjamin D. Foulois took off from the grass parade field at Fort Sam Houston in San Antonio.

Lt. Foulois had taken a correspondence course in flying and transferred to the Signal Corps in hopes of convincing the army to get into aviation. His break came when the Wright brothers wrecked one of the airplanes they had built and offered to sell the pieces to the government for $1,500. Both the pieces and Lt. Foulois were sent to Texas to reassemble and fly the Wright Type "A" biplane.

After weeks of patching the thing together, Foulois was ready to take to the air. He made four flights the first day. On the final trip, a fuel line broke and the plane made a rather bard landing breaking the rudder and almost knocking him out of his seat. After all, the plane had achieved the unbelievable speed of fifty miles an hour. Foulois made the first military innovation by adding a seat belt. He also insisted the skids be replaced with wheels.

It took less than sixty years after that for us to put a man on the moon and even less time than that for the greatest addition to aviation, the pretty stewardesses on airline flights.

TEXAS WEATHER

When Jan and I first moved onto our little ranch, we placed a used mobile home up on the hill to live in while we built our dream house. It took longer than we thought and Jan complained that she wouldn't spend another summer in that hot trailer. God heard her and sent a tornado to blow it away with us in it. Son, Andy, leaped in the bathtub when we saw it coming. Jan and I just had time to hit the floor beside him. When it was all over, Andy was still in the tub, but it was on its side on the ground. The bathtub at the other end of the mobile home was found a mile away in a tree. Andy just happened to get in the right bathtub. Jan and I walked away without a scratch. People told us how lucky we were. Of course I told them if I had any luck at all, I wouldn't have been hit by a tornado.

Texans boast about everything, even about our weather extremes. We point to how hot it gets, 120 °F in places in 1936 and 1994 and how cold it gets, -31 °F in 1899 and 1936. Texas averages more tornadoes than any other state. Back in the winter of 1923, the town of Romero received 65 inches of snow.

Blue Norther

If you have lived in Texas long, you probably know what we mean by a "Blue Norther." That is when you see dark blue clouds coming in from the north and you know you are in for a drastic temperature change, sometimes as much as a hundred degrees in a few minutes.

One Texas cowboy, not being into exaggeration, described his experience this way: "I was out mending fences when a blue norther blew up suddenly. Having a good horse, I decided to outrun it. I put my mount into a fast gallop and the horse began to sweat. By the time I reached the barn, the front end of the horse was lathered up and the back end was frozen over."

The worst blizzard to hit Texas in recorded memory came on February 13-14, 1899. Within hours temperatures dropped to the lowest the state had ever seen. In the panhandle the mercury dropped to 31 below zero, 23 below at Abilene, 16 below at Denison, 11 below at Dallas, and 4 below at San Antonio.

The San Antonio River was frozen over so thick folks were walking on it. Port Aransas shivered at 5 above. People walked on the harbor ice. Parts of Corpus Christi Bay were frozen over.

During the drought of 2011, someone sent an email claiming:

A buddy out of Longview said he'd killed a mosquito that was carrying a canteen.

A man in Dime Box said the chicken farmers were giving the chickens crushed ice to keep them from laying hard-boiled eggs.

In Lake Palestine they caught a 20 lb. Catfish that had ticks on it!

But just this week, in Bryan, TX, a fire hydrant was seen bribing a dog.

It's so dry in Texas that the Baptists are starting to baptize by sprinkling, the Methodists are using wet-wipes, the Presbyterians are giving out rain-checks, and the Catholics are praying for the wine to turn back into water.

Now THAT'S DRY!

BURIED TREASURE

Everyone knows about Texas bank robbers and killers, Bonnie and Clyde, but few remember the four Newton brothers, Willis, Willie, Jesse, and Joe. These enterprising Texans went on a crime spree that lasted over half a century. The brothers robbed eighty seven banks and six trains. They got away with more money than the Dalton Gang, Butch Cassidy's Wild Bunch and the James-Younger Gang combined.

In 1910 Willis was caught trying to steal a 600 pound bale of cotton he couldn't carry. He was sent up the river for two years.

Later, Willis and his three brothers began robbing banks, trains, and post offices. When Texas got too small for them, they moved north into Oklahoma, Kansas, and Illinois. In 1924, they pulled off their crowning achievement by robbing a train and making off with the greatest haul in United States train robbery history up to that time. Within days, they were rounded up and sent to prison.

Crime was a way of life with these guys. In 1968, 44 years after the great train robbery, Willie got bored living in a rest home and was brought in for robbing a bank.

But here is where the buried treasure comes in. Their cousin, Tim Newton, tells the story of a time back in the 1920's when the brothers pulled a heist in Oklahoma and returned to Texas. They rounded up cases of booze, four shady ladies, and moved into a house where they engaged in some serious debauchery. It soon occurred to them that if the cops caught them with all their ill-gotten loot, it might incriminate them. So one night they took a large part of it and drove west out of San Antonio on a dirt road till they came to a field full of white rocks. They rolled one back, dug a hole, threw in the treasure and returned the rock on top of it. Then to mark the rock, they all peed on it.

Later, when they went back to retrieve the treasure, they couldn't remember which dirt road they took out of town. They were never able to find their treasure. So here is your chance to get rich. Just look somewhere west of San Antonio for a field of large white rocks. Look for one that has been peed on. How hard could it be?

DUST BOWL

My wife, Jan, had an older sister she never met because she died while still a baby from dust pneumonia in the 1930's Dust Bowl.

For centuries natural grasses held the topsoil in place in Kansas and the Oklahoma and Texas panhandles. Then in the twentieth century the grass was turned under to make way for farming. Land was stripped bare. When the drought hit in the 1930's nothing grew and there was no root structure to hold the soil in place.

As if the great depression was not enough, now the area was turned into a dust bowl. There were fourteen severe dust storms in 1932, thirty eight in 1933, and one hundred thirty four in 1937.

On May 9, 1934, a major "Black Blizzard" started in Montana and by night dumped 6,000 tons of dust on Chicago. By next morning it had reached New York where street lights came on at midday. In the spring of 1935, people began to die of dust pneumonia and natural grasses were being planted to save what top soil was left. It was estimated that 850 million tons had blown away.

By 1940, two and a half million people had left the plains states. The rains came again in 1939 and conservation practices were in place. The drought in the 1950's was not such a disaster.

THE GREAT DEPRESSION OF THE 1930'S

My friend Jane Cheatham tells of her experiences growing up on a farm in the 1930's. Her family lived three and a half miles from town, but somehow the word had spread that they never turned the hungry away. A Hobo would walk all the way out there and ask if there was any work he could do for food. Jane's mother might find some little chore for him while she scraped together some leftovers. Then while he ate, she would fix whatever she could for a lunch to send him on his way. Though they were poor, they never said no.

The federal government set up the CIVILIAN CONSERVATION CORPS (CCC) from 1933 to 1942 giving young men some employment while jobs were near impossible to find and money was scarce. This gave outdoor work for 2.5 million men ages 17 to 25 from families on relief. They were paid $30 a month. $25 of it was sent directly to the family. At its peak, 19,200 men in Texas were employed in camps of 200 to build state parks or work on soil conservation projects.

My father took a correspondence course in radio repair. He set up shop in Corpus Christi. He had moved the family to Texas figuring if we were going to starve, at least we would do it where it was warm. Somehow he managed to put enough food on the table to keep us alive. When World War Two broke out, the economy began to move again. Even so, Texas with its oil industry was about the best place to be during the depression.

RED RIVER BRIDGE WAR

The Red River Bridge Company had been operating a toll bridge between Durant, Oklahoma and Denison, Texas, serving U.S. Routes 69 and 75. Texas and Oklahoma then jointly built a new, free bridge northwest of the existing toll bridge.

July 10, 1931, the Red River Bridge Company obtained an injunction against the Texas Highway Commission restraining them from opening the new bridge. The company said the highway commission had promised to buy the toll bridge for $60,000. In reaction to the injunction, Texas Governor Sterling, ordered the new free bridge be barricaded from the Texas end.

July 16, Oklahoma Governor Murray ordered the new bridge open, by Executive Order on the grounds that the land on both sides of the river belonged to Oklahoma, per the Louisiana Purchase Treaty of 1803. Murray sent highway crews across the new bridge to destroy the barricades.

Governor Sterling sent Adjutant General William Warren and three Texas Rangers to the new bridge to defend the Texas Highway Commission workers enforcing the injunction and to rebuild the barricade. The next day, Oklahoma crews under Governor Murray's order demolished the Oklahoma approach to the toll bridge, rendering that bridge impassable.

July 23, the Texas state legislature called a special session to pass a bill allowing the Red River Bridge Company to sue the state over the issue. The next day, Governor Murray declared martial law at the site, enforced by Oklahoma National Guardsmen. A Muskogee, Oklahoma court issued an injunction prohibiting him from blocking the northern toll bridge approach. Murray directed the guardsmen to allow anyone to cross either bridge.

Murray discovered on July 27 that the free bridge was in danger of being closed permanently. He expanded the martial law zone across the river, stationing guardsmen on both free bridge approaches. The injunction against the bridge opening was dissolved and the martial law order rescinded on August 6. War with Oklahoma was averted. It is good they didn't have the bomb back then.

The free bridge that was the cause of the dispute was opened on Labor Day, September 7, 1931.

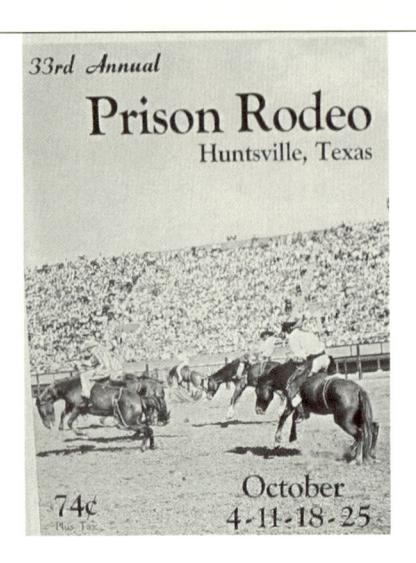

TEXAS PRISON RODEO

In the depression era 1931, times were hard. The Texas prison system was strapped for money to operate like everyone else.

The general manager came up with the idea of a prison rodeo with the inmates as contestants.

It started out slow with only a few prison employees and locals coming to watch, but it grew into the biggest sporting event in Texas, attracting as many as 100,000 fans.

The rodeo eventually went on the road where entertainers such as Johnny Cash and Dolly Parton performed as well.

Then in 1986, for reasons I can't understand, they shut it down. It was a government operation, and who can understand government logic?

"I'm Douglas Corrigan. I just got in from New York. Where am I? I intended to fly to California."

Douglas Corrigan

WRONG WAY CORRIGAN

Douglas Corrigan was born on Galveston Island in 1907. When he was 18 he got the bug to learn to fly. He was working for Ryan Airlines in San Diego, California when Lindberg contracted Ryan to build an aircraft to fly across the Atlantic. Corrigan helped build it.

He later nurtured a dream of flying solo across the Atlantic himself. By 1933 he bought a second-hand OX5 Robin plane for $325 and modified it for a flight to Ireland. It took two years saving his money for extra fuel tanks and other add-ons. In 1935 he requested permission from the FAA to make the flight. He was turned down. He spent another two years making more modifications costing an additional $600. The Feds continued to deny his request saying the plane was not safe for the trip.

On the morning of July 17, 1938 he filed a flight plan from New York to Long Beach, California, only once in the air, he headed east until he reached Dublin, Ireland 28 hours later.

Not wanting to lose his pilot's license, he claimed it was equipment failure.

He was an instant sensation. He had defied the bureaucrats and won. Corrigan returned to New York to a ticker tape parade and WRONG WAY CORRIGAN became a house-hold word.

The Feds knew when they were beat. They suspended his license for two weeks which was about as long as Corrigan's boat ride back to the States. Until the day he died, he swore it was all a mistake caused by a faulty compass.

One out of every 4 personal vehicles in Texas is a pickup truck.

I think Texans have more fun than the rest of the world.
Choreographer Tommy Tune

TEXAS WON WWII

When the United States gets itself into a messy war, they turn to Texans to dig them out. After the Japanese raid on Pearl Harbor at the beginning of World War Two, they turned to a Texan, Admiral Chester Nimitz for leadership by putting him in charge of all the fighting forces against the Japanese.

Upon given authority by President Roosevelt, he flew to Hawaii to assume command. There was a general feeling of defeat and despair. After viewing the destruction of the U.S. Pacific Fleet at Pearl Harbor, he was asked what he thought. Admiral Nimitz said the Japanese made three big mistakes. They made the attack on Sunday while nine out of ten crewmen of those ships were ashore on leave. If those ships had been lured to sea and sunk—we would have lost 38,000 men instead of 3,800. The Japanese got so carried away sinking our ships; they overlooked the dry docks nearby. We would have had to tow every one of those ships to America for repair. All the fuel in the Pacific is in top of the ground tanks five miles away. One attack plane could have destroyed our total fuel supply, but they did not. The Japanese made three of the biggest mistakes an attack force could make. With this positive, can-do Texas attitude, Nimitz took charge and was soon dealing death blows to the Japanese.

Toyko Bay—Surrender of Japanese aboard USS *Missouri*. Admiral Chester Nimitz, representing the United States, signs the instrument of surrender.

While Nimitz was whipping up on the Japanese during WWII, another Texas born warrior, Dwight David "Ike" Eisenhower was the big Kahuna over all allied forces in defeating the Germans and Italians in Europe. Succeeding in that, he was elected the 34th President of the United States.

To help Ike out in Europe during WWII, he sent over Mrs. Murphy's boy, Audie, who ended up the most decorated soldier in WWII. He demonstrated to the troops how we used to deal with the Comanche. Starting out as a private, he continued to get battlefield promotions until he ended up the war as a Lieutenant. Below is some of what the reports say about Murphy.

Following its participation in the Italian campaign, Murphy's 3rd Division landed in Southern France. Shortly thereafter, Murphy's best friend, Lattie Tipton, was killed by a German soldier in a machine gun nest. Murphy went into a rage and single-handedly wiped out the German machine gun crew who had just killed his friend. He then used the German machine gun and grenades to destroy several other nearby enemy positions. During seven weeks of fighting in a campaign in France, Murphy's division suffered 4,500 casualties. He was hit in the hip by a sniper's ricocheting bullet and spent ten weeks recuperating. Within days of returning to his unit, and still bandaged, he suffered further wounds from a mortar round which killed two others nearby.

The next day, January 26, the temperature was 14 °F with 24 inches of snow on the ground. It was during the battle at Holtzwihr, France. Murphy sent all of his men to the rear while he took pot-shots at the Germans until out of ammunition. He then proceeded to use an abandoned, burning tank destroyer's .50 caliber machine gun to cut into the German infantry including one full squad of Germans that had crawled in a ditch to within 100 feet of his position. Wounded in the leg during heavy fire, he continued this nearly single-handed battle for almost an hour. As his remaining men came forward, he quickly organized them to conduct a counter attack, which ultimately drove the enemy away from Holtzwihr. For these actions Murphy was awarded the Medal of Honor.

One must take the suggestion to heart, "Never hit a Texan while he is down. He might get up."

HELIUM

Helium is #2 in the periodic table of elements with two electrons in each atom. It is twice as heavy as Hydrogen that only has one, but only a third as heavy as oxygen or nitrogen which make up 99% of the atmosphere. Thus a balloon filled with helium will float in the air.

When the Hindenburg crossed the Atlantic, it was filled with Hydrogen because the Germans had no helium. Trouble is, Hydrogen burns while Helium is inert, ergo the disaster when the giant airship caught fire upon reaching America.

Helium was first discovered on the sun rather than on earth when someone aimed a spectroscope at the sun during a solar eclipse and noted the distinctive Helium footprint.

Helium was found in the Texas oil fields as a byproduct of natural gas. When they tried to burn off the gasses escaping from the drilling operation they found it would not burn. On investigation they determined they had Helium.

During World War Two, German U-boats were ravaging American shipping along our coasts. The Navy stationed a fleet of Helium filled blimps along the shores to track down the submarines. The blimps couldn't go fast, but they could stay aloft for a week at a time.

I was stationed in Georgia in the Navy in the late nineteen fifties where they had the last training facility for blimp crews. At the time, these lighter than air ships were being phased out. They had outlived their usefulness.

One winter day, blimp pilots filed a flight plan for a trip to New Jersey. They took off early in the morning. There was a north wind. All day long we could see the blimp slugging into the wind. Come evening it was still in sight of the field. The crew gave up and returned for landing, deciding to try again another day.

The Navy needed Helium to fill the blimps so a Helium storage facility was set up outside of Amarillo, Texas. A billion cubic meters of the gas was stored there at the Cliffside Storage Facility.

Over forty years after the last blimp was decommissioned, the government decided maybe it was time to get out of the Helium business and turned Helium collection and refining over to the private sector. This was pretty efficient by government standards. It took only forty years to shut down an unnecessary program. Most government programs never die. Today, the lion's share of refined Helium in the world is right here in Texas near Amarillo.

A NEW KIND OF BURIED TREASURE

During WW II, the army established Camp Maxey outside of Paris, Texas. It served as a training facility and prisoner of war facility. When the war was over, they dismantled the camp and were faced with what to do with all the military hardware. Dumping the jeeps and guns on the open market would create hardship for the auto and arms manufacturers. The government solution was to bulldoze huge pits, throw in the tanks, jeeps, flame throwers, rifles, machine guns, bazookas, etc. and cover them over. Fire arms were put in barrels and preserved in cosmoline.

There is a fortune in arms if anyone knew where to dig on the seventy thousand acres that once was Camp Maxey.

Think of it. Dig it up, dust if off and you have an instant army. Just add thirty thousand soldiers.

Dr. John Brinkley

DEL RIO RADIO

There must be something about Del Rio, Texas that attracts fruit cakes like Judge Roy Bean and Doctor John Brinkley.

Doctor Brinkley got his medical license through a correspondence course. When Kansas ran him out, he came to Texas and hung his shingle in Del Rio across the Rio Grande from Mexico. Actually his shingle was radio station XER, a powerful voice that could reach the whole lower 48 United States. Mexico did not limit the power of the broadcast and that is where XER's antenna is located.

Brinkley made his fortune hawking his patent medicines and a male potency procedure involving a sliver of goat testicle inserted into libido-challenged men for $200.

The world lost one of the truly great quack doctors when Brinkley died in 1942 but his legacy lived on. I remember hearing Del Rio radio late at night when I was going to school in Illinois in the early 1950's. For a nominal fee one could order an autographed picture of Jesus Christ or a wind-up doll of John the Baptist that would pop its head off on demand.

They say the broadcast signal was so strong even the barbed wire fences would pick it up and people could sometimes hear music from the fillings of their teeth.

Texas is the crossroads of the world. Everything here is big.
Bobby Lee

TEXAS IS A STATE OF MIND

Texans view themselves not as Americans living in Texas, but as Texans living in America.

"There is a growing feeling that perhaps Texas is really another country, a place where the skies, the disasters, the diamonds, the politicians, the women, the fortunes, the football players and the murders are bigger than anywhere else."
Brooklyn journalist Pete Hamill

The Founding Fathers of America were statesmen, religious leaders, and philosophers. The Founders of Texas were people who fought too much, drank too much, and womanized too much.

Texas was once an independent republic and it has experienced an uneasy marriage with the United States. From time to time we see Texans calling for a separation. The love for independence has never gone away. Though the ten years of Texas sovereignty saw war and massive debt, some Texans long to dissolve the bond with the United States.

Recently Richard McLaren founded "The Republic of Texas" (ROT). At first, he opposed federal taxes, but then he got to reading legal history and decided the United States never legally annexed Texas at all. No one complained about this when it actually mattered in 1845. Somehow, he convinced a group of people that his argument was valid.

McLaren issued liens and judgments for trillions of dollars. He lobbied the United States for recognition as a sovereign country and tied up courts slowing down real estate transactions across the state. Then he wrote millions of dollars' worth of bad checks. Not a good idea.

By 1997, the ROT had split into two factions. McLaren led the smaller more violent group. The more peaceful side decided McLaren had gone too far when his group kidnapped Margaret Ann and Joe Rowe in retaliation for the arrest of two ROT members who were driving without state license plates.

McLaren ordered members of his militia to begin picking up federal judges, legislators, and IRS agents for immediate deportation. This was the last straw for Texas law enforcement. Almost 300 state troopers and Texas Rangers laid siege to the ROT at Ft. Davis, Texas. One member of the ROT was killed, and a hostage was wounded in the standoff. McLaren was sentenced to 99 years in prison for the kidnapping and standoff and an additional 12 years for 26 counts of mail and bank fraud.

Supporters of the idea of an independent and sovereign Texas are still around, although they have prudently refrained from firing officials who impose state and federal laws.

Governor Rick Perry once responded to shouts from the crowd calling for Texas to secede. *"There are a lot of different scenarios,"* said the Governor. *"We've got a great union. There's absolutely no reason to dissolve it. But if Washington continues to thumb their nose at the American people, you know who knows what might come out of that. But Texas is a very unique place, and we're a pretty independent lot to boot."*

ANNA NICOLE SMITH

Vickie Hogan dropped out of school in the eighth grade and took odd jobs in fast food and Wal-Mart. She married Billy Smith when she was seventeen, had a son, got divorced, and hired on as a stripper in a club in Houston. Here she took advantage of her greatest asset. She was "drop dead beautiful:." Vickie took on the name of Anna Nicole to add a little class. Then she met 88 year old Howard Marshall II, the richest man in Texas. In May of 1992 she was Playboy's Playmate of the month. Now she really had class. "If you've got it, flaunt it."

At 26, Nicole married Marshall but he died fourteen months later. At his advanced age, Marshall was unable to take full advantage of his new acquisition, but he sure had bragging rights. There wasn't much action around the house so Nicole went on a shopping spree, chalking up six figure monthly credit card bills. Isn't it nice to see a little hometown Mexia, Texas girl enjoy herself?

Marshall left everything to his son, Pierce, and his "grieving widow" sued for half her husband's estate. The tabloids got a lot of mileage out of the case. Anna Nicole Smith Marshall ended up with only $88.5 million out of the estate of her husband's $1.6 billion and the family appealed even that. The court case lasted longer than the marriage. That is life in the fast lane in Texas. She died later of an overdose of drugs. What a shame. No telling how far she could have gone if she had only finished high school.

REPTILES

One June, a six foot alligator showed up in a little pond on our 50 acre spread in East Texas. We called the fish and wildlife guy (Hank) to help us deal with him. Come to find out some people want alligators. I guess they keep an infestation of dogs and children down. Folks put their name on a list, and as alligators are caught they are taken to those who want one.

Our pond was hardly more than a puddle, only twelve feet across. Hank had a pole with a steel wire noose on the end he hoped to loop around the gator's nose, but that lizard wasn't buying it. He submerged himself and wouldn't resurface. I produced a rotten minnow net and with me on one end and Hank on the other, we drug our quarry up on the bank. Hank suggested we get him away from his element (water), so we tried to drag him further up the bank.

A neighbor, driving by, had stopped to see what we were up to. Somehow he got between the gator and the water when that critter exploded through the net and headed back to the pond flapping his jaws. It scared the neighbor pretty bad. He suddenly remembered he needed to go home, and I haven't seen him again in the years since.

Hank and I drug the pond again and got the beast to the edge of the water. We knew if we tried to drag him further he would repeat his escape as before. For the moment we just stood there with the gator defiantly hissing at us. That is when the hired lady got the wire noose around his nose and we had him.

SNAKES

There are four kinds of poisonous snakes in Texas: coral snakes, copperheads, cotton mouth moccasins, and rattlesnakes. I share all four on my little piece of paradise plus a number of other varieties of snakes.

We had a hog-nose snake out in the blueberry patch. I would come across him from time to time and he always gave me a little start since he was small and colored somewhat like a copperhead. But then I would notice his turned up nose and I would mess with him. He would flare his neck out like a cobra. When that didn't scare me, he rolled over and played dead. I would roll him over on his tummy and he would roll back on his back and play dead again.

I figure most snakes are beneficial so I leave them alone, but it is nice to be able to tell the good guys from the bad. There is a king snake that likes to emulate the coral snake with bright red, yellow, and black stripes. I can tell the difference because the coral snake has the red and yellow stripes adjacent to each other. The king snake has the red and black adjacent to each other. Just remember, "Red and yellow kill a fellow, red and black venom lack." Coral snakes are the most venomous, but they have a small mouth and can hardly bite. Besides they are extremely rare. I have never seen a live coral snake, just a dead one on the road in front of our place.

The other three venomous snakes are pit-vipers. They can be recognized by their triangular shaped heads and the pupils of their eyes are slit instead of round.

Shortly after we moved to the country from Dallas, Jan and I were swimming in the little seven acre lake in the back yard. A cotton mouth swam over to check us out. He stopped about six feet away and looked us over. Jan was nervous till I explained to her that we were obviously no threat to the snake and we were too big to eat. We were not in any danger. Then the snake went under water where we couldn't see him and we promptly got out. Haven't been swimming in that lake since though the kids and grandkids have enjoyed it.

My friend, Bill, was in the middle of a separation from his wife when he was bitten by a copperhead. His wife suddenly remembered that she hadn't paid the last installment on his life insurance. She left him there and went into town to pay it. Vindictive the lady was. My sister, Nancy, was bitten by a copperhead, and grandson, Bradley, by a cotton mouth. All three survived just fine. If we do get bitten, chances are we will not die. It was always the snake they didn't see that bit them. Snakes will likely get away from you if they are given a chance. Imagine what a snake must think when he sees a human. Here we have hands and feet to fight with. A snake is basically a stick with a mean mouth. He can only slither. If I were a snake, I wouldn't like the odds. I keep the place mowed and the snakes find someplace else to be where they can hide.

RATTLESNAKE ROUND-UP

On the second weekend in March every year the Jaycees in Sweet Water, Texas sponsor a Rattlesnake Round-up to raise money for charity. It is the largest such event in the world. For over half a century, contestants have vied to see who can bring in the most rattlesnakes. A crowd of over thirty thousand comes to view the goings on.

Outside the huge coliseum an animal rights group pickets, protesting the practice of such cruelty to these not-so-lovable critters. Inside, one can watch the milking of the snakes. The venom is used for medical purposes. Cooks make a killing selling deep-fried rattlesnake meat. Other vendors sell snake skins for hat bands, rattler key chains. Stuffed and mounted snakes are for sale if you fancy one for a centerpiece on the dining room table. I don't remember how many pounds of rattlesnakes were brought in when I attended. The record year was just under nine tons. It is not as if they are going to run out of rattlesnakes. It averages about the same every year.

THOSE ARE RATTLESNAKES THE SNAKE QUEEN IS WADING AMONGST
THE GIRLS MUST RUN TO THE DOOR TO AVOID ENTERING THAT BEAUTY CONTEST

Center stage at the round-up is a snake-pit consisting of four foot high panels fastened together to form a circle maybe fifteen feet across. Into the pit, snakes are turned loose and a couple of handlers walk around among them. I believe these are usually guys. Most ladies have better sense. A table stands in the center of the pit. I watched the man pick up a snake and place it on the table. The old rattler had already developed an attitude after being hauled out of his home and brought in. Then the handler aggravated him to coax him to strike. One wonders how many times these guys got bit before they learn just how close they can be and still avoid taking a poison fang in the hand.

Though I didn't witness it, I understand they once had a contest to see who could stuff the most rattlesnakes in a gunny sack in a given amount of time. Maybe they had to discontinue the practice because they were losing too many contestants.

For a fee, attendees can go on a hunt to see how they catch these vipers. Gasoline is sprayed to flush the snakes out from their lairs beneath large rocks.

Though the reptiles might disagree, it is all for a good cause, a spectacle uniquely Texas.

For those planning to immigrate to Texas, I would advise you learn the language, such words as "ya'll" is the plural of you. Fixin' to indicates an intention to begin doing something.

It may take years, but in time immigrants slowly morph into real Texans. They will find themselves sending out emails claiming outlandish creatures were shot near Conroe, Texas, and making unbelievable pronouncements like, "Texas won world wear two".

BLUEBONNETS

Life becomes a drag if we don't stop to smell the flowers along the way. Only Texas can boast the grand bluebonnet spectacle that graces our roadsides in the spring. A man has no poetry in his soul if he doesn't stand in awe at the sight. The Texas hill country is the best place to view them. The best place is the Willow City Loop. Take highway 16 north out of Fredericksburg and look for the Willow City sign. On a good year the loop becomes a fairy land ablaze in color. For the best time and places to see the Texas wild flowers go to the website,

www.lone-star.net/wildflowers/willowcityloop.htm

Texas is neither southern nor western. Texas is Texas.
Senator William Blakley

FERAL HOGS

It is estimated there are four million feral hogs in the United States and half of them live in Texas. They are so destructive there is a bounty on them. Females can produce two litters a year averaging six per litter. The hog population can double in four months.

These porkers ravaged our place and destroyed my corn crop this year. Traveling in packs, they can root up several acres in a night and dig as deep as three feet. They are mostly active after dark so I seldom see one.

Some months ago, I bought a trap five by five by eight feet of heavy wire. I baited it with corn and waited eagerly for my first opportunity to have a pig roast. The crows ate the corn and I never caught a hog. Someone told me that if I soak the corn in diesel fuel, the pigs will eat it, but nothing else will. Pigs will eat anything. So I soaked the corn in diesel and still had no luck. Pigs are smart and trap savvy.

Grandson, Bradley, saw where they had been rooting down by the lake and he moved the trap down there. He caught a beaver. It seems beavers will eat diesel soaked corn as well as hogs. Bradley coaxed the irate beaver out of the trap and reset it. The second time he caught the beaver, he had a really angry beaver on his hands, so Bradley moved the trap away from the lake.

When I was based on the Georgia coast in the Navy, one of the helicopter pilots rigged a wire loop on the end of a long pole and was catching feral hogs out in the marshes till the game warden spotted him and called our commanding officer. The pilot was grounded from flying the helicopter. I confined my helicopter pursuits of pigs to just harassing them. Flying the helicopter was too much fun to risk being grounded. It is not unusual to see these hogs weighing over four hundred pounds. A pig roast could feed all my friends and some people I don't even like very well. I continue hunting them.

CADDO LAKE

Caddo Lake has been called the most beautiful lake in America. It is the largest natural lake of fresh water in the south, covering about 26,800 acres and features the largest cypress forest in the world.

Half the lake is in Texas and half in Louisiana. The lake was formed by a 100-mile long raft of trees that backed up the Red River.

Ecologist Lionel Janes surveyed Caddo Lake in 1914. Based on the cross sections of bald cypress and hardwoods he claims the lake formed between 1770 and 1780.

According to Caddo Indian legend, the lake originated in the 1812 New Madrid earthquake. The lake was probably there, but got much bigger as a result of the quake which inundated a large Caddo Indian settlement on the banks of the original lake.

Just prior to the earthquake, the chief had a vision and warned his people to get out. He led many to a nearby hill. Those who chose to stay perished.

All my life I have heard about the "wild west," but there was never any place as wild as the shores of Caddo Lake in the early 1800's. The Spanish claimed Texas and the French claimed Louisiana. The dividing line between the two was somewhat in question. The area became a haven of lawlessness. The region known as Old Monterey on the shores of Caddo Lake was the center for racetracks, rooster fights, saloons, and brothels, and boasted an average of a murder a day. Travelers were ambushed, robbed, and murdered when the criminals weren't killing each other.

In 1840 Sheriff Alfred George enlisted Charles Jackson to help him resolve an issue with Joseph Goodbread. Jackson solved the problem by murdering Goodbread. Jackson was arrested, but released awaiting trial. While waiting, Jackson formed a vigilante group called the Regulators to clean out the den of outlaws. Then the Regulators got so abusive an opposing group, the Moderators, was formed to reign in the Regulators. War broke out between the two groups resulting in battles, armed forts, and cannon fire. What would you expect in Texas?

The trial of Jackson for the murder of Goodbread was scheduled for July 12, 1841. Judge John Hansford would be the presiding judge. The Judge was a friend of Goodbread and a known supporter of the Moderators. The Regulators believed Jackson was not apt to get a fair trial. They came armed to the courthouse. Judge Hansford, seeing the mob, declined to hold court. He left town. The Moderators then killed Jackson and the Regulators retaliated by burning down the homes of two of the Moderators.

Charles Watt took control of the Regulators. Under his command, the Regulators got so large and powerful that Watt considered taking on the Republic of Texas. He figured he could win and declare himself dictator of Texas. That never happened, but Judge Hansford who refused to try Jackson in fear of his own life was eventually murdered anyway.

In 1844, President Sam Houston sent a group to East Texas to bring peace to the region. Ten leaders from both sides were arrested, brought in to negotiate a settlement and dissolve both the Regulators and the Moderators. This put an end to the conflict.

Paddleboat and steamboat traffic through Caddo Lake thrived in the 1830's – 1840's carrying iron ore, cotton, leather goods, and people. The port of Jefferson was second only to Galveston as a port city and was far larger than the little towns of Dallas and Ft. Worth.

Jay Gould came to Jefferson building a railroad. He demanded they give him land to run tracks down the middle of Austin Street. When the city fathers declined, he put a curse on the city, declaring grass would grow on the streets. Jefferson would die without his railroad. In 1873, after the civil war, the Federal government in its "great wisdom," removed the Great Raft of the Red River. The water level in Caddo Lake dropped. This terminated steamboat travel on Caddo Lake and Gould's prediction came true.

A new economy boomed, fresh water pearls, but the pearling industry had a short life. It ended when the first dam on Caddo Lake was built.

No lake anywhere holds a higher diversity of native aquatic life. There are more than 90 species of fish and 20 species of mussels native to the lake. Make a point not to die without taking a cruise among this spectacular beauty. I suggest boarding the Graceful Ghost, a replica of an 1800's era steamboat. It is a live steam driven vessel with a working paddle-wheel and wood fired boiler. The two hour journey worms its way silently among majestic cypress trees draped in Spanish moss.

People who visit Caddo Lake will tell you that one word is not enough to describe it. They use words like magical, enchanting and delightful.

The Graceful Ghost tours Caddo Lake
Tuesday through Friday at 12 pm,
2 pm & 4 pm. On Saturdays the tours are
10 am, 12 pm, 2 pm and 4 pm.
1-877-894-4678.

I done drew the line. Just like the Alamo. You're either on one side of the line or the other. I don't want to ever leave Texas again.

Former Houston Oilers coach Bum Phillips

LOVING COUNTY COURTHOUSE

LOVING COUNTY

In his book, TEXAS, AMAZING BUT TRUE, Jack McGuire tells of the county with "the most of the least." Loving County, half the size of Rhode Island, is 473 square miles of nothing, with a population of 64. Here one finds no natural drinkable water. The Pecos River that started out as a clear mountain stream has long since turned bad in its trek south. There is no railroad, bus station or airport and fewer than 30 miles of roads. Mentone, the county seat, is the only town. It boasts a courthouse, gas station and combination café and beer hall. The last birth was recorded a half century ago. It is the most sparsely populated county in the lower 48 states. Though there is no church or pastor, crime is unknown. The one jail cell remains empty. Wells have been dug all over the county and never yielded water, only oil. School kids, both of them, are bussed to Wink, Texas. With so few roads, it is 154 miles round trip. If you ever get a chance to visit Loving County, pass it up and take another cruise on Caddo Lake.

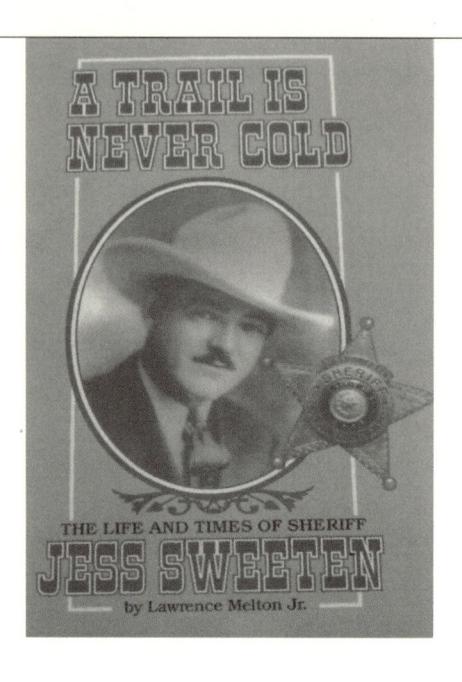

SHERIFF JESS SWEETEN

Jess Sweeten was quiet spoken, well dressed, polite and thoughtful, but he was also six foot four inches of solid muscle who never lost a fist fight or a shoot-out. There never was a murder or a rape he couldn't solve. He was the law in Henderson County and the most popular sheriff in all the United States, the kind of Texan we all think we are.

Picture Trinidad, Texas, during early days of the great depression. Population, 250. Mud streets. There was a new highway coming through town and a large electric power plant under construction introducing electricity to rural East Texas. Trinidad was suddenly a boom town with 1,500 transient workers looking for diversion every evening. Aunt Lillie's whorehouse never prospered so well and the bootlegger on the corner sold sour mash whiskey. Illegal slot machines supplied by a local lawyer graced the walls of the pool hall.

Scrap Iron Johnson, a huge bear of a man stood in the middle of the street peeing into a mud puddle and making lewd advances to ladies passing by.

Now they had gone too far. Foghorn Holliday, the new deputy constable was determined to show he was up to the job. He went out and pistol whipped Johnson as hard as he could several times about the head. Johnson didn't go down. Holliday holstered his gun, walked to the café, and turned in his badge. He wasn't up to the job.

Joe Dyer, the night watchman for the railroad tried to carry the mail pouch from the Post Office to the depot which brought him too close to the bully in the middle of the street. Johnson and a couple of his buddies decided to have sport with him. When Dyer couldn't reason with the men, he pulled out his gun. Johnson took it away from him, knocked him down and mopped the street with Dyer pulling him back and forth through the mud.

Jess Sweeten was in town to catch a train bound for his new job in Kansas City as a steel worker. He had seen enough of the abuses of Scrap Iron and his friends. He walked over and told Johnson to give the man back his gun. When Scrap Iron hesitated, Jess knocked him clear into next week. When Johnson woke up days later, he had a broken jaw and six missing teeth.

The city fathers observing the affair knew they had found their new constable if they could convince him to take the job. They offered him $140 a month plus room and board. Besides that, he would get $4 for every arrest he made. Jess thought hard about that. This was the depression where no one had any money. $140 was a good salary. Looking down the street there were at least a hundred arrests he could make right then. That would be $400. He took the job.

Thus began the law career of Jess Sweeten who quickly went from deputy Constable to Deputy Sheriff to Sheriff. It is all chronicled in Lawrence Melton's book, THE TRAIL IS NEVER COLD, THE LIFE AND TIMES OF SHERIFF JESS SWEETEN.

Jess was an innovator. Arresting law breakers one at a time and caring them to the sheriff in the county seat was too slow and cumbersome. He rented a cattle car from the railroad, got hay for bedding from a local farmer, and provided pee pots from the general store. This was Trinidad's new jail. The first day Jess fought twenty fights and arrested over a hundred men. Aunt Lillie retired and moved to Dallas. The battle of Trinidad, Texas was won.

If you read books, set your eyes on Melton's. It is a cliff hanger that reads like a novel. In his last life, Jess must have been a Texas Ranger.

TEXAS HAS ITS OWN POWER GRID

The United States electricity supply system consists of three power grids, the Eastern Interconnection, the Western Interconnection, and the Texas Interconnection. The Lone Star State has its own power grid partly because of a historical desire for self-sufficiency and the independent Texas attitude. A small section in west Texas and a few in far north-east Texas are not on the grid, but 85% of Texans get their electricity from the Texas grid.

The local utilities have pledged not to sell their power to interstate customers. As a result, the interconnection is exempt from most regulation by the Federal Regulatory Commission. This resistance to federal regulation plays well where meddling from Washington, D.C., is generally abhorred. The state uses more electricity than any other, 44 percent more than runner-up California.

Managed by the Electric Reliability Council of Texas (ERCOT) Texans appreciate their independence. They also keep their eye on the bottom line and anything that gives them a competitive business advantage. Texas is different from the nation for a lot of reasons.

Go to either of the other two grids and you've got to get twenty-something approvals to get anything done. In Texas, there is only one to persuade. As a result, Texas has quickly erected enough wind turbines to become the national leader in wind-energy by a wide margin. As an independent nation, Texas would rank sixth in wind power in the world. With a semiconductor industry already based in Austin, Texas could do the same with solar. Texas is a major technology center. If it decides to lead, it is well positioned to.

Texas now generates about 8500 megawatts of wind energy (three times as much as California) and has completely maxed out the existing transmission capacity. Plans call for $5 billion worth of new transmission lines to carry electricity from Texas's most remote areas to its urban centers. These lines will increase the system's transfer capability to 18,000 megawatts.

TEXAS INDEPENDENCE

Richard McLaren isn't the only one who recently pushed for Texas independence. Daniel Miller heads the Texas Nationalist movement. He believes Texas can merely declare its independence and walk away from the union without firing a shot. Pointing to the economic disaster United States law makers have manifested, Miller is convinced Washington is broken beyond repair. They have wandered too far from the original Constitution to ever return to sanity. He doesn't advocate breaking any laws or taking up arms. He just wants Texans to understand how much better Texas would be if it was independent.

When Texas was an independent republic in the 1830's and 40's she was poor and threatened. Today if she was independent she would be the seventh largest economy in the world.

Texas is a little larger than France.

Texas refines over 85% of the gasoline in the United States.

Over 65% of the defense industry is based in Texas.

Texas has enough oil and natural gas to supply its needs for the next 300 years.

Texas produces more cattle, more horses, and more wool than any other state and half the mohair for angora sweaters in the world.

Texas leads the nation in producing computer chips and electronics.

Texas Instruments, Dell Computer, EDS, Raytheon, National Semiconductor, Motorola, AMD, ATMRL, Applied Materials, Ball, Dallas Semiconductor, Delphi and Nortel are based in Texas.

Texas balances its budget while Washington has forgotten how and asks Texas to bail it out.

Texas has the largest centers for cancer research, the best burn centers and the top trauma units in the world.

Texas boasts essential control of the U.S. Paper, plastics, and insurance industries.

Texas is self-sufficient in beef, poultry, hogs, grain, fruit, vegetables, and sea food.